BOLD NOT
BELLIGERENT

A CHRISTIAN'S RESPONSE
IN A FALLEN WORLD

PETER DEMOS

FIVE
STONE
PRESS

Romulus, Michigan

FIVE
STONE
PRESS

FiveStonePress
Every Book a Giant-Killer
An imprint of Supernatural Truth Productions, LLC
www.FiveStonePress.com

Endorsement

Peter Demos explores what true biblical boldness looks like. His thoughtful and thorough treatment of the subject not only inspires and emboldens, but it also offers strategic and effective solutions to confronting a belligerent and often times Antichrist social construct that seeks to shout us down and endeavors to drown out dissenting opinions. Peter's timely book encourages true biblical Christianity in the face of what is now called progressive Christianity to boldly, prayerfully, and powerfully stand against the onslaught of SJW imposters who have endeavored to hijack the Word of God and, thus, the church. Peter takes no prisoners, holds no hostages, and in a refreshing and respectful way, teaches us how to engage with culture while seeking to bring glory to the name of Christ Jesus.

Shane Ogle
Lead Pastor, Great Lakes Church
Sterling Heights, Michigan

Foreword

Peter Demos masterfully distinguishes between boldness and belligerence. As followers of Christ, we are called to navigate a fine line between these two attitudes—a line that, if misunderstood, can undermine our witness to the world. Peter emphasizes that boldness, when rooted in God's grace, empowers us to stand firm in truth, speak with love, and live out our faith with humility and courage. In contrast, belligerence, fueled by offense or other ulterior motives, blinds us to grace and can turn us into defenders of our own pride instead of ambassadors of Christ.

In this book, Peter Demos invites you to embrace your identity in Christ as someone who is saved, called, and destined to live boldly. This is not a call to be contentious or abrasive but rather to step into the fullness of God's purpose for your life—one that is grace-filled, truth-bearing, and love-abounding.

The pages ahead are filled with compelling stories, personal reflections, and scriptural insights that further illuminate this essential distinction. From the biblical accounts of apostles who transformed the world with fearless faith to modern examples of believers facing complex cultural challenges, the narrative encourages you to reflect on your walk with Christ.

Through relatable experiences and a conversational tone, the author guides us in leaving behind the temptation to fight fire with fire and instead fanning the flames of grace-fueled boldness. This book will challenge you to examine your heart, evaluate your actions, and ensure that your faith is expressed in ways that honor God and attract others to him.

Whether you've grappled with the tension between standing

firm and remaining humble or you are simply seeking encouragement to live out your faith boldly, this book will inspire and equip you. It reminds us that true boldness in Christ is not loud or combative; rather, it is unshakable, confident, and ultimately driven by acts of love.

Prepare to be challenged, encouraged, and compelled to act. The journey ahead will deepen your faith, refine your perspective, and empower you to live as the bold, grace-filled believer you were created to be.

Kevin McGary
EBLM, Cofounder
www.EveryBLM.com
https://locals.com/member/DEIGUY

Table of Contents

CHAPTER 1

Be Bold and Not Belligerent

In September 2021, I published my book *On the Duty of Christian Civil Disobedience*. Since then, I've had to defend my position that civil disobedience is not limited to protests. At times, I have had people refuse to take the book at all, thinking civil disobedience refers to aggressiveness or being obnoxious. Others will reluctantly take it when I press the point about what it really means.

Let me be completely clear. My worldview comes from a Judeo-Christian perspective. This motivates me as to how I see the world and my response to it. To see the world from the philosophies that have failed us and respond in the same way is not the way to be successful in standing up against the world or for the gospel.

In our society, people clearly don't know what it's like to be bold in the face of culture without acting like a fool. In essence, many people seem to confuse boldness with belligerence.

The social norm today is to see people screaming at each other. Sometimes they behave this way face-to-face, and other times, they act this way on social media. The yelling tactic has been used for many years. It's nothing new.

When we look back on the Civil Rights movements in the South, we see photos or videos of loud, shouting racists who thought their ranting would stop integration. They screamed at the silent protestors on the other side.

One of my favorite paintings by Norman Rockwell is titled

"The Problem We All Live With." The painting depicts a six-year-old African American girl, Ruby Bridges, walking to school accompanied by US Marshals. Ruby Bridges became a symbol of the desegregation of public schools. She is shown in her white dress, holding a small notebook, her face set in calm determination. The US Marshals in dark suits walk beside her for protection as she heads to the newly desegregated William Frantz Elementary School in New Orleans.

The background of the painting is stark and deliberate. It features a wall with racial slurs and the remnants of a thrown tomato, emphasizing the hostility and resistance Ruby and other African American students faced during the desegregation era.

Which of these two approaches do you view as bold? Ruby at the center and the marshals flanking her? Or the belligerence of the crowd she walks by?

For some reason, even when we consider examples like this, we conflate boldness with obnoxious, loud behavior. And if this is not an accurate view of boldness, then what is, and how do we avoid belligerence?

The internet has plenty to say on the matter. A quick search brings up countless articles on bold leadership and the traits of bold individuals. Some define boldness as fearlessness in the face of danger, while others see it as a willingness to act despite uncertainty or risk. Both views highlight important aspects, but boldness, in its fullest sense, is more than just confidence or risk-taking. It is the strength to move forward with clarity and conviction, even when the outcome is unclear.

I can sit on my couch, confident I'm willing and fearless—at least, I can do this when the risks are small. We can easily imagine we would be bold in dangerous circumstances. But later, when we are confronted by those dangers, our boldness fades away.

You may see someone who is bold in how they dress, bold in how they stand for the right thing, bold against bullies or cruelty. These are all possible. And yet, when you look at those who are belligerent, often, you see these same traits. Unfortunately, they are still defined as boldness.

On the other hand, belligerent behavior is defined as being hostile or aggressive. Boldness is often included in this definition as well. However, as Christians, what are we called to? We are called to be bold—but not necessarily aggressive or hostile.[1]

We have to look at what it actually means to be bold and add our own definition based on biblical character. Christian boldness is the action of standing up. It requires we get the job done or we protect or promote a person or idea despite the risks and consequences. Further, we accept these potential consequences without violence or hostility, and we do so with humility. Boldness is not belligerence or bravado. However, boldness may mean raising your voice in order to engage in self-defense or in the defense of others.

Where belligerence is aggressive or prone to attack others by nature, it is rooted in pride or even idolatry. We can easily scream at those who are different when our emotions are high. We can throw things at them, insult them, or treat them poorly in other ways. The reality is that hiding behind our emotions or the emotions of a particular groupthink is not boldness or standing up for others. It's hiding.

With all the examples of belligerent expressions in our culture today, where do we see the examples of bold Christians who are actually standing and accepting the risks?

Jaelene Daniels

The North Carolina defender made a name for herself in women's soccer. Despite her career with professional teams and even in the Olympics, Jaelene was unwilling to compromise her faith. When her team required its players to wear a pride jersey to promote the LGBTQ[2] lifestyle, she refused to do so based on her religious

---

[1] Let's be clear that this does not deal with a Christian's duty of self-defense or approach the idea of just war, even though it is often seen as aggressive behavior.
[2] Determining what to call this community is challenging. I have seen it labeled as "LGBTQQIP2SA," "LGGBDTTTIQQAAPP," or the more culturally prevalent "LGBTQIA+." Princeton not only suggests using "LGBTQIA+" but also emphasizes we should practice saying it out loud. They propose changing the term to "the proper one," which varies, depending on usage within the community. (The Trustees of Princeton University, "LGBTQIA+ 101," Gender + Sexuality Resource Center, Princeton University, accessed May 18, 2025, https://www.gsrc.princeton.edu/lgbtqia-101.) Wikipedia's "List of gender identities" far exceeds 100 entries, Tumblr has listed 112 genders and 70 sexual orientations, and Medicine.net catalogs 72 genders. Consequently, I will refer to

beliefs.

She missed multiple opportunities due to her refusal to wear a pride jersey. Jaelene did not throw a fit. She didn't organize any protests or rally others to her side. She didn't scream at the club owner. Instead, Jaelene simply said no.

Violating her Christian beliefs wasn't worth it, and she was willing to miss out on the pay and prestige of her career. As a result, her contract was not renewed.[3]

Paige Casey

As a nurse practitioner, Paige worked for CVS Pharmacy. Due to her stance on the God-given sanctity of life, she was unwilling to fill prescriptions for abortion medications. Initially, when Paige wrote a letter to corporate headquarters requesting an accommodation for this belief, CVS Pharmacy granted it and accepted this conscientious objection.

However, she was later fired and told she couldn't have the accommodation.

Paige's refusal to do something she believed was wrong led to a loss of income and even her career reputation. Her willingness to accept this consequence reflects boldness. She didn't do anything big and dramatic. She didn't throw away the drugs. She didn't shame those who came for the medication. She didn't try to stage a walkout. Paige simply said she couldn't do it and followed through even when it meant termination.[4]

Isabel Vaughn-Spruce

---

this group as simply "LGBTQ," excluding the "+" because, as Princeton explains, the plus sign represents the "expanding and new understanding of different parts of the very diverse gender and sexual identities." Since I do not believe LGBTQ identities are divinely ordained genders, I will use these five letters as representing the community advocating for political and social transformation. However, I do not recognize these identities as natural or in line with divine creation.

[3] Joel Brown, "NC Courage Player left off roster after refusing to wear pride jersey on Pride Night," July 29, 2022, ABC11 Raleigh-Durham, https://abc11.com/nc-courage-pride-night-celebration-lgbtq-player-refuses-to-wear-jersey/12084013/.
[4] Olivia Diaz, "Nurse practitioner says CVS fired her over objection to abortion drugs," September 2, 2022, *The Washington Post*, https://www.washingtonpost.com/dc-md-va/2022/09/01/cvs-nurse-fired-abortion-pills/.

The fact is abortion is a matter of moral ground for many, but Isabel Vaughn-Spruce is another woman who showed boldness in the face of mounting pressure. What did she do?

Silently prayed.

Isabel did not say anything or hold a sign. She didn't shout at the women entering the clinic. Instead, she stood outside and silently prayed, knowing God hears her and He is the One who can bring a change to the hearts of those who seek to end the lives of their children.

For this seemingly simple act, Isabel was arrested not once, but twice. One might expect her to have stopped her silent prayers on the sidewalk after the first arrest, but Isabel would not be deterred. She was arrested a second time, although she was cleared of all charges from the first arrest weeks earlier.[5] Although Isabel accurately explained she was not protesting, the police told her everyone knew why she was there. They knew what she was doing. This act was enough to warrant her arrest.[6]

Are You Bold?

We can easily think we are not brave when we compare ourselves to people like those listed above. Maybe those sacrifices seem too much for us to bear. Maybe risking a job loss would send our family spinning into poverty or an arrest for a thought crime could disqualify us from a goal we are working toward.

Christians in the US will often say, "I am not bold." I hear it from people all the time. But I completely disagree with that. I think all humans have the ability to be bold, especially when we are pushed to a point where it's the only option or when we are truly passionate.

Consider the boldness people show when it comes to their favorite football teams. They will go to the opposing team's hometown game while wearing their own team's colors, knowing it will upset others, but confident as they support the team they love.

---

[5] EWTN, "Pro-Life Woman Arrested in the UK Again for Praying Outside Abortion Clinic | EWTN News Nightly," March 9, 2023, YouTube, http://www.youtube.com/watch?v=3NyGoDm4Lbs.

[6] Kevin J. Jones, "Woman arrested for silent prayer at UK Abortion Clinics gets police apology," September 22, 2023, NCR, https://www.ncregister.com/cna/woman-arrested-for-silent-prayer-at-uk-abortion-clinics-gets-police-apology.

They are proud of where they stand. They don't have to be belligerent and instigate issues with the opposing team; they're simply demonstrating where their support lies.

People also tend to get bold when it comes to green lights. Think about how often you find yourself at a red light behind a couple of other cars. Suddenly, the light turns green. But the driver in the front at the intersection just . . . sits. He or she doesn't move. Maybe they got distracted by the helicopter flying overhead, or they decided to use the red-light moment to respond to a text, or they're busy telling their child in the backseat that they can't have a snack until they get home. But the longer you sit there, the more insistent the honks become. Usually, the noise alerts the driver right away, but sometimes the other drivers feel the need to step out in boldness, shall we say, and keep a hand on the horn as long as it takes.

In reality, whether sticking to your busy schedule or declaring your loyalty to a sports team, boldness often depends on the context and where your passion lies. The idea we're not naturally bold is, simply, a lie.

Think about how often people will become bold when it comes to justice issues. If their child is being bullied, they will do what they feel is best to end the trouble. They may give their child the tools to stand up, but they will often also approach the parents of the other child or, in the case of a school setting, discuss the issue with leadership to put boundaries in place on campus.

Was there ever a time when you put in great effort on a project, but you got a poor grade even though you know you deserved better? Or your boss didn't respond positively?

Oftentimes, this will spark the boldness to respectfully address the issue and find the core of the matter while defending your stance and your work.

These are just a few examples of areas where people often find their boldness in everyday situations. It doesn't require a dramatic move, and there doesn't have to be a life-altering consequence. Sometimes it's about the little things. But people do stand up. We are capable of boldness.

The Bold Christian

Christians need boldness all the time but especially in our

current day and culture. We need this boldness for two main reasons. First, we need to protect ourselves. As our country moves further away from God, Christians are being labeled as dangerous extremists and even called domestic terrorists. This is a slippery slope—a slope I don't want to see in my lifetime. More than that, I pray it won't continue down this path for my children and grandchildren in the future.

Christianity has been directly called out in reference to the January 6, 2021, riots that took place at Capitol Hill. Reports from *The Atlantic*, *NPR*, and *The New Republic* all suggest that Christianity was responsible for the violence that took place that day, while many others infer a link to Christian nationalism.[7] Moreover, the Southern Poverty Law Center has declared the Alliance Defending Freedom (ADF) a designated hate group, frequently calling them extremists.[8]

But the attacks against Christians don't end there. From personal to political, in private and in public, Christians are daily facing waves of hostility for our faith. A weak, malleable version of Christianity can be praised as loving and social-justice oriented, whereas true, biblical Christianity is scorned for its doctrines regarding sin and the need for God's justice, righteousness, mercy, and grace.

What is the second reason we need to step out in boldness right now? As Christians, we must be bold because we love our fellow men and our country.

We see throughout the Old Testament that Israel walked away from God time and time again. And whenever they did, God judged them. He incited their enemies to rise up against them. We see this with the Assyrians, the Babylonians, and the Romans, all conquering

---

[7] Emma Green, "A Christian Insurrection," *The Atlantic*, January 8, 2021, https://www.theatlantic.com/politics/archive/2021/01/evangelicals-catholics-jericho-march-capitol/617591/; Tom Gjelten, "Militant Christian Nationalists Remain a Potent Force, Even after the Capitol Riot," *NPR*, January 19, 2021, https://www.npr.org/2021/01/19/958159202/militant-christian-nationalists-remain-a-potent-force; Matthew Sutton, "The Capitol Riot Revealed the Darkest Nightmares of White Evangelical America," *The New Republic*, January 14, 2021, https://newrepublic.com/article/160922/capitol-riot-revealed-darkest-nightmares-white-evangelical-america.

[8] "Alliance Defending Freedom: SPLC Designated Hate Group," Southern Poverty Law Center, accessed May 16, 2025, https://www.splcenter.org/resources/extremist-files/alliance-defending-freedom/.

Israel. Likewise, God will judge us. And rather than viewing this as a reason to institute Christianity as a national religion when historically that has only harmed the church and given further power to corrupt leaders, we can see it is a greater reason that those who are in Christ must influence culture and love our neighbors through our boldness.

We want to ensure people understand the true source of freedom. As Christians, we know freedom comes through our enslavement to Christ. We want to demonstrate life in Christ isn't about the next five to ten years. It is about the next hundred years of society and about life with Christ eternally.

Unfortunately, the lack of boldness in my generation and those that came before has led to a distorted view of culture. A distortion of good can only be described as evil.

Where do we see insane ideas in our culture today?

Gender-Affirming Care: I and many others would call this gender mutilation. This is not happening simply in consenting adults but even in children who are, by nature of youth and development, confused about gender identity and are sold a lie before they are old enough to understand the consequences of the decision they are manipulated into making.

Hannah Faulkner rightly says that the very term *gender-affirming care* refers to the affirmation of the gender God gave them.[9]

Abortion Tourism: Tourism once referred to traveling for the purposes of relaxation or education. It consisted of going to museums and looking at striking art from past centuries or sites of historic importance.

Now states advertise their abortion-friendliness, welcoming women from states that have strict rules on terminating their pregnancies. In essence, they promote the tourist attraction of coming to their cities so that a woman can kill her baby. Many of these states, or at least their defenders, have even advocated for so-called abortion up to twenty-four hours after the baby is born—but this is actually infanticide. Whatever the lies told about a child in the

---

[9] Producer, "Teens against gender mutilation rally & report on DCS with State rep. Mike Sparks and guests," January 26, 2023, WGNS Radio, https://www.wgnsradio.com/article/79170/teens-against-gender-mutilation-rally-report-on-dcs-with-state-rep-mike-sparks-and-guests.

womb, even a fully birthed baby is now at risk of being murdered—although they use the term *after-birth abortion* to minimize the language and the seriousness of their actions.[10]

Violence: Unrelenting violence across the nation is reaching alarming and increasingly normalized levels. While violence in schools is not new—tragically, isolated incidents have occurred throughout US history—the frequency, intensity, and public awareness of such attacks has grown significantly in recent decades. Forty years ago, few would have imagined that active shooter drills would become a routine part of elementary education or that school architecture would include defensive design features. Today, we send our children to institutions that must prioritize security training from the earliest grades on. The nature of the threat, the cultural attention surrounding it, and the systemic preparation it now demands mark a dramatic shift from the past.

Cokeville Elementary School in Wyoming experienced a horrific explosion when David and Doris Young decided to bring in a bomb, due to David's belief he would be a god in his brave new world and the children would be happier there. He also believed he would manage to bring in a ransom for each child before blowing up the bomb, granting himself riches for the reincarnated life. David was delusional, but miraculously, only he and his wife, Doris, died. The children and teachers all survived the explosion, despite a number of injuries and burns.

After the event, those who had been crammed into the small classroom reported they prayed, and many claimed to have seen angels protecting them.[11]

But David Young's violence was not for the sake of violence but was rather a plan based in a false reality.

Today, many school and church shootings are not born out of these motives and this kind of madness. They are born out of a desire to hurt people, to bring pain. They are meant to punish others or

---

[10] Alberto Giubilini and Francesca Minerva, "After-birth abortion: Why should the baby live?" *Journal of Medical Ethics*, 39, no. 5 (2013): 261–3, https://jme.bmj.com/content/39/5/261.

[11] Jessica Clark, "Cokeville Elementary School bombing," November 8, 2014, WyoHistory.org, http://www.wyohistory.org/encyclopedia/cokeville-elementary-school-bombing.

make a name for themselves.

As these instances seem to continue and increase, often the perpetrators are young and hurting. In a society where isolation and self-involvement are prominent, young people seem to resort to violence, often born out of frustration and the entitlement that they should have what they want.

The motivations behind acts of violence—particularly among younger individuals—are deeply troubling and increasingly complex. While manifestos and personal writings often reveal a sense of alienation or unresolved identity conflict, the growing trend of individuals seeking affirmation through extreme measures raises serious concerns. In a few recent cases, individuals identifying with LGBTQ+ labels have been involved in violent incidents, though details often emerge slowly and must be treated with caution.[12] The broader issue is not about one community but about a culture that fosters confusion, isolation, and anger—and fails to offer meaningful, truth-centered connection and hope.

Major Institutions

We live in a time when even major institutions approve of evil and make allowances for behaviors we have fought to reject as a nation.

Although marriage laws vary from state to state, many rules about the age of marriage and the age of consent to sexual activity are meant to protect children. These laws have developed over time and have shifted here and there in order to prevent abuse and to stigmatize those who have perverse proclivities toward children.

But movements such as the minor-attracted-persons orientation are just a way to numb the public to the fact that these people are nothing more than pedophiles. As we'll examine more closely, the changing of definitions and manipulation of words is a tactic often used to twist morality. This movement that once hid in the dark corners of Twitter and has continued since the transition to X has also begun to be more widely accepted.

Even the major social institutions are approving of evil.

---

[12] Aleks Phillips, "How Many Mass Shootings Have Been Carried Out by Transgender People?," Newsweek, March 28, 2023, https://www.newsweek.com/mass-shootings-transgender-perpetrators-1790854.

Media: In 2022, *USA Today* published an article initially titled "What the Public Keeps Getting Wrong about Pedophilia."[13] While the backlash prompted a change in title and the originally tweeted thread was deleted, the article was never removed. Instead, they doubled down on the argument that pedophilia is a sexual orientation someone may have. But if it is not necessarily acted upon, therefore, it should not be labeled as child abuse.

In truth, Hollywood promotes all levels of sexual immorality, from premarital sex to extra-marital sex, from casual sex to homosexual sex and more. Media like *Pretty Little Liars*, winner of multiple Teen Choice awards; *Brokeback Mountain*, winner of three Oscars; and *Lolita*, both the original and remake, winner of awards for best newcomer; and *American Beauty*, winner of eight Oscars, all fall under the rather broad category of film or television that normalizes various types of underage attraction.

But why should sexuality and relationships be taken more seriously? Culture has diminished the permanency of committed, unconditional love, so why would we expect anyone to continue high standards in their romantic affections?

We still read the story of Lot and his daughters in Genesis 19 and are horrified (Genesis 19). This father offers his daughters to be raped only for them to turn around and eventually assault him in his drunkenness. We consider it primitive culture or just plain gross. But what we see promoted in the media today is no less horrifying when we really think about it.

Family: Divorce rates have increased significantly since the 1960s, unironically the same decade when birth control, pornography, and more extreme forms of feminism exploded. The rates of divorce peaked in the 1980s. Since Covid hit in 2020, however, reports show divorce is on the downward decline, with only a slight uptick in 2024.[14]

---

[13] Lindsay Kornick, "USA Today torched for promoting 'complicated' study on pedophilia," January 11, 2022, Fox News, http://www.foxnews.com/media/usa-today-blasted-promoting-complicated-pedophilia-study.

[14] Jaden Loo, "Divorce rate in the U.S.: Geographic Variation, 2022," Bowling Green State University, 2022,

Although this decline in divorce rates seems like promising news since the days of lockdown when families were forced to spend more time together, the family is still under attack. The number of unmarried couples living together has increased, and the practice has gained cultural acceptability. In fact, 59 percent of people have cohabited with an unmarried partner. Of eighteen to twenty-nine-year-olds, 78 percent surveyed believed it was acceptable for a couple to live together outside of marriage—even if they didn't plan on getting married.[15]

For adults aged thirty to thirty-nine, one in four are currently living with a partner they aren't married to.[16] We have to ask if the divorce rate is dropping due to committed relationships or if it's dropping simply because fewer people are getting married.

When 65 percent of adults don't believe premarital sex is a moral issue and those choosing to wait for marriage are dwindling, it's no wonder our view of marriage and romantic commitment has deteriorated.[17] In the past, sex was reserved for within marriage—or stigmatized and shamed when practiced outside of marriage. In the past fifty years, casual sex increased through visits to bars and clubs. For those who didn't manage to meet anyone in person, *Playboy* and other sexual publications filled the gap. But recently, technology has created such rapid outlets for sexual appetites that we shouldn't be surprised by these changes.

No one needs to go buy a magazine anymore. They just type their proclivity in the search bar. And if someone wants casual sex that evening, they can opt for hookup sites or apps that clearly state what they're looking for. In the United States, the prevalence of these sites and apps is increasing. Traditional dating sites were designed as a solution for long-term relationships that hoped to end in marriage.

https://www.bgsu.edu/ncfmr/resources/data/family-profiles/loo-divorce-rate-US-geographic-variation-2022-fp-23-24.html.

[15] Juliana Menasce Horowitz, Nikki Graf, and Gretchen Livingston, "Marriage and cohabitation in the U.S.," November 6, 2019, *Pew Research Center*, https://www.pewresearch.org/social-trends/2019/11/06/marriage-and-cohabitation-in-the-u-s/.

[16] Francesca A. Marino, "Age variation in cohabitation, 2022," Bowling Green State University, 2022, https://www.bgsu.edu/ncfmr/resources/data/family-profiles/marino-age-variation-cohabitation-2020-fp-22-28.html.

[17] Derek Hales, "Which countries are the most promiscuous?" NapLab, October 23, 2024, https://naplab.com/guides/which-countries-are-the-most-promiscuous/.

Now these sites have nearly been replaced by those looking to connect for purely sexual purposes.

According to *Marriage.com*, "Unlike committed relationships, casual relationships prioritize independence, flexibility, and mutual enjoyment without the expectation of exclusivity or long-term commitment. They often involve physical intimacy, but the emotional connection is typically less intense and exclusive."[18] Sites like Ashley Madison and many others don't simply provide a hookup for two consenting adults. They specifically target married adults who want to engage in discreet affairs.

Truly, the institution of marriage and family is under attack, sometimes even from within.

Economy: Even the economy in the United States is not immune to the evils of the age.

Drugs have created an economic boom and have been quite a blessing to fund the CIA and other operations. Books, magazine and newspaper articles, documentaries, and more have confirmed this, and the Department of Justice has even posted this information on their website.[19] Plenty of questions surround what happens to the money and drugs confiscated during sting operations, and we probably won't get any straightforward answers to those questions.

But drugs aren't the only thing being trafficked around this nation. Human trafficking is at an all-time high with quiet slavery seeping in all over the country. From sex tourism, most often run by pimps and other traffickers, to illegal immigrants and minorities used as domestic and sex labor, human trafficking is rampant.

We can look back to the 2015 Trans-Pacific Partnership (TPP) negotiations to see how the US was willing to manipulate a nation's human trafficking status for economic gain. Under the US State Department's Trafficking in Persons (TIP) report, countries are ranked based on their efforts to combat human trafficking. **Tier 3 is** the lowest ranking, reserved for countries that neither meet the

---

[18] Christiana Njoku, "What Is a Casual Relationship? Types, Risks & Benefits," Marriage.com, September 4, 2024,
https://www.marriage.com/advice/relationship/casual-relationships/.
[19] "The CIA-Contra-Crack Cocaine Controversy: A Review of the Justice Department's Investigations and Prosecutions," accessed May 16, 2025,
https://oig.justice.gov/sites/default/files/archive/special/9712/ch01p1.htm.

minimum standards for eliminating trafficking nor make significant efforts to do so. **Tier 2**, by contrast, is for nations that fall short of those standards but are making tangible, good-faith efforts to improve. Malaysia had been listed as Tier 3 due to its serious trafficking problems, which should have excluded it from participating in the TPP under US law. However, just before the final deal was reached, Malaysia was controversially upgraded to the Tier 2 Watch List—despite no substantial evidence of reform. This allowed the trade deal to proceed, raising serious concerns among human rights advocates that the TIP report was being politicized, undermining its integrity in favor of economic and diplomatic interests.[20] What are the lives of those trafficked worth in the face of America getting cheaper imports?

Another example of engaging in evil for economics' sake is PornHub. Not only have some women, including minors with featured assaults, made numerous accusations and taken legal action against the company, but they don't use age-verification for viewers due to the financial loss they would face.[21] It simply isn't worth it to them to ensure viewers are above eighteen.[22]

While these are only a very few examples, they demonstrate what we're told in 1 Timothy 6:10, "For the love of money is a root of all kinds of evils. It is through this craving that some have wandered away from the faith and pierced themselves with many pangs."

If economics can be used to justify evil in a culture, someone will find a way to do just that.

Education: Unfortunately, our educational system is not even

---

[20] Avi Asher-Schapiro, "Is the US ignoring human trafficking abuses to score its TPP trade deal?" *VICE*, July 17, 2015, https://news.vice.com/en_us/article/xw3xva/is-the-us-ignoring-human-trafficking-abuses-to-score-its-tpp-trade-deal.

[21] Laila Mickelwait, "Pornhub's Senior Manager was caught confessing the reason they won't verify age is because they would lose '50% of traffic' and 'it costs money,'" X, November 29, 2022, https://x.com/LailaMickelwait/status/1597626867338870784.

[22] Laila Mickelwait, "This was a Pornhub senior manager confessing why they refuse to implement age verification—they don't want to lose money. These predatory sites won't change," X, January 3, 2023, https://x.com/LailaMickelwait/status/1610356148057804800?lang=en.

immune to the wickedness of the day.

In 1962, prayer was removed from schools through the Engel v. Vitale case.[23] Schools could no longer recite prayers or require students to do so. While we live in a country that has the freedom of religion and some families understandably have differing religious views, this ruling initiated a dramatic shift.

A year later, in 1963, the Supreme Court said public schools cannot sponsor Bible readings and recitations of the Lord's Prayer.[24] At the time, many people were angry about it. Republican officials campaigned in support of reinstating prayer in schools, addressing it as a moral issue. But within two years, the passionate disagreement lost steam, and the subject was simply forgotten.

Within a few years, the sexual revolution was born, and in ten years, *Playboy* reached its peak in global circulation in 1972 with more than seven million readers, continuing the downward spiral of culture that appeared to have stemmed from the removal of one staple practice that held morality as a forefront for children when it was needed.[25]

Although this is one example of the correlation that stemmed from the removal of God from public schools, we can also see the reverse is true. In Ukraine, a Bible-based elective called *Christian Ethics* was introduced in select regions, not as a government mandate but as a voluntary curriculum designed to reintroduce biblical values to students. As this program expanded, government officials noticed something remarkable—*test scores increased and disciplinary problems declined* in the areas where the Bible was being taught. When President Poroshenko inquired about the cause, the Minister of Education reported that these improvements correlated directly with the implementation of Christian Ethics courses. Though Poroshenko was not a believer, he recognized the measurable benefits and called for

---

[23] "Facts and Case Summary - Engel v. Vitale," US Courts, accessed May 16, 2025, https://www.uscourts.gov/about-federal-courts/educational-resources/educational-activities/first-amendment-activities/engel-v-vitale/facts-and-case-summary-engel-v-vitale.

[24] "Abington School District v. Schempp, 374 U.S. 203 (1963)," Justia US Supreme Court, accessed May 16, 2025, https://supreme.justia.com/cases/federal/us/374/203/.

[25] Josh Sanburn, "Brief History: Playboy," *Time*, January 24, 2011, https://time.com/archive/6595160/brief-history-playboy/.

the elective to be offered throughout the entire nation.[26]

As we've already examined, violence in schools has also increased significantly.[27] It's not just teens and adults going on shooting sprees for various reasons. But students and their own angry responses to one another and toward faculty are creating this culture.[28]

Playboy was the pornography king of the 1960s and '70s and eventually became more hardcore like *Hustler* and *Penthouse*, which then graduated to home videos. Some movies celebrated Larry Flint of *Hustler* as a hero, and these can now be easily streamed without even showing an ID.

Now books with pornographic images and graphic written descriptions of sexual acts sit in school libraries, including in elementary and middle schools, for students to access whenever they like.[29] Those who take issue with these materials in schools are accused of book banning and are told they are a part of the problem and might as well be communists. They're compared to the overlords in *The Handmaid's Tale* as if their authoritarian nature is to be feared if we don't hand our children these books. Some of the sex acts described are so graphic that when parents try to read sections at school board meetings to address the issue, they are told they cannot read explicit material in that setting.[30]

---

[26] Dirk Smith, interview by Peter Demos, *Uncommon Sense in Current Times*, recorded June 9, 2025, podcast, air date TBD.

[27] Stephen Sawchuk, "Violence in schools seems to be increasing. Why?" November 1, 2021, Education Week, https://www.edweek.org/leadership/violence-seems-to-be-increasing-in-schools-why/2021/11.

[28] F. Chris Curran and the Conversation, "School kids are so violent coming out of the pandemic that they're sending teachers to the hospital, but an expert says to resist 'get tough' approaches," September 24, 2023, *Fortune*, https://fortune.com/2023/09/24/why-high-school-students-violent-dangerous-pandemic-solutions-discipline/.

[29] Max Eden, "Do These Books Belong in Public School Libraries? You Be The Judge | Opinion," Newsweek, May 26, 2023, https://www.newsweek.com/do-these-books-belong-public-school-libraries-you-judge-opinion-1802689.

[30] Christopher Tremoglie, "Moms for Liberty exposed this graphic content in elementary school libraries," *Washington Examiner*, July 24, 2023, https://www.washingtonexaminer.com/opinion/2213067/moms-for-liberty-exposed-this-graphic-content-in-elementary-school-libraries/.

Religion: All this leads us to what is, perhaps, the most disturbing of all: one of the culpable institutions approving of this evil is none other than the church. You might expect this to be the greatest bastion to protest against culture. You would expect that the church would never give in to the evils of culture.

Throughout Scripture, we see the constant theme of culture's conflict with righteousness and God's justice. The Bible is clear about the division between being "in the world" and not "of the world." And yet, even this major institution has begun the culture drift and is approving of evil.

Progressive or woke Christianity is on the rise. Rather than biblical Christianity that seeks to influence culture, progressive Christianity is a lie influenced by culture. The idea is that we must use culture to somehow attract and bring people into the church. We use affirmation so they can learn about a loving God. We use approval so we don't scare them away.

This is exactly what Paul warns Timothy about, having a form of religion, while denying its power. This deception not only infiltrates seekers in these so-called churches but is even motivating those who previously claimed to hold biblical values to rethink their views. While there are many theological implications as far as whether or not these people were ever truly in Christ, we can clearly see the New Testament warnings.

The church is warned to be wary of false teachers and false prophets. And yet, we see how insidiously these dangerous leaders have crept in anyway.

Out of laziness, many self-proclaimed Christians would rather listen to their pastor and ignore their Bible than to challenge themselves and seek truth. Reading the Bible requires the motivation to see what God actually says and if that lines up with what their pastor says or not. If it doesn't line up, they would have to seek a new church family, and they would have to take the Bible seriously— even when it's not convenient.

When living a sinful life, people don't want to turn away from their wrong behaviors and repent. Instead, they try to find places that will support their view—and their sin—even if those behaviors disagree with God. Churches that affirm these acts are looking for new members and believe the quantity of members matters. They see value in the validation they not only give but receive from sinners who openly flaunt a sinful lifestyle and believe this is proof they're doing what they should.

From there, they add arguments from the pulpit disproving the Bible so that they can get away with teachings that don't align with God. And this simple formula is all it takes for a religion to promote evil, even in the name of Christianity.

There are numerous examples of priests and preachers who have molested children, assaulted women, promoted the LGBTQ lifestyle, or promoted other forms of immorality that run counter to the holiness God wants for his people. They even instill these people as leaders in the church, promote their marriages, and encourage the confused to indulge their confusion. They praise the trans ideology and go beyond just the sexuality issue.

They will use ideas of critical race theory and oppression to fuel division—all in the name of compassion and tolerance. Where the Bible declares there is no Jew nor Greek, slave nor free, these leaders grasp at Marxist ideology as a means of political approval. They completely ignore that it really pushes the idea that minorities are incapable of succeeding until a so-called privileged person lets them. They promote the thought that a person's skin color or immigration status is more important than the person's identity in Christ, which causes greater damage.

Biblical Boldness

Proponents of these ideas want to say the Bible is all about love, and therefore, we should love one another as our primary objective. While it is correct the Bible urges us to love one another, this love is not at the expense of being bold. The Bible demands truth and encourages us to stand up against sin. Nowhere in the Bible are we instructed to love Satan and all he promotes. Nowhere does the Bible tell us to love his demons. Nowhere in Scripture does it say to approve of evil.

The Bible encourages us to use boldness, showing that it's a mark that we are empowered by the Holy Spirit. The Holy Spirit gave boldness in the New Testament, demonstrating his power. We see this in Acts after Pentecost when the apostles go out, preaching the gospel. In Acts 13, Paul in Antioch says:

But when the Jews saw the crowds, they were filled with jealousy and began to contradict what was spoken by Paul, reviling him. And Paul and Barnabas spoke out boldly, saying, "It was necessary that the word of God be spoken first to you. Since you thrust it aside and judge yourselves unworthy of eternal life, behold, we are turning to the Gentiles. For so the Lord has commanded us, saying, 'I have made you a light for the Gentiles, that you may bring salvation to the ends of the earth.'"

We can look to these men and see how they stood up in the face of the false leaders. We know the Bible tells us to stand and, for that purpose, we must do just that. We have to stand against evil. But how can we stand against a culture that is crashing without showing boldness? We can't. And the Bible supports this through many verses.

Put on the whole armor of God, that you may be able to stand against the schemes of the devil. For we do not wrestle against flesh and blood, but against the rulers, against the authorities, against the cosmic powers over this present darkness, against the spiritual forces of evil in the heavenly places. Therefore take up the whole armor of God, that you may be able to withstand in the evil day, and having done all, to stand firm. (Ephesians 6:11–13)

"Resist him, firm in your faith, knowing that the same kinds of suffering are being experienced by your brotherhood throughout the world" (1 Peter 5:9). "Therefore, my beloved brothers, be steadfast, immovable, always abounding in the work of the Lord, knowing that in the Lord your labor is not in vain" (1 Corinthians 15:58).

How can we argue with the Bible? How can we, like those progressive leaders who use the love of God as an excuse for sin, justify ourselves in being nice instead of bold? We are urged to put on the armor of God—with the boldness of soldiers. We are urged to resist Satan, even when it's hard and we suffer for it. We are urged to be steadfast and immovable in our dedication to the things of God.

The Bible is rife with these examples, and we see them time after time. We know God desires for us to live according to his will. While the above verses paint a clear picture, they're only a small selection. We see this call to boldness again and again through phrases like "steadfast" and "standing firm."

"Only let your manner of life be worthy of the gospel of Christ, so that whether I come and see you or am absent, I may hear of you that you are standing firm in one spirit, with one mind striving side by side for the faith of the gospel" (Philippians 1:27). "Be watchful, stand firm in the faith, act like men, be strong" (1 Corinthians 16:13). "Therefore, my brothers, whom I love and long for, my joy and crown, stand firm thus in the Lord, my beloved" (Philippians 4:1).

From the Old Testament to the New Testament, this is the pattern. People like Noah stood firm and built the ark, despite the taunts and mocking. Joseph fled Potiphar's wife even at risk of imprisonment. They did what was right, no matter the cost. And, ultimately, whether in this life or not, those who stand firm will see justice and experience true freedom.

"For freedom Christ has set us free; stand firm therefore, and do not submit again to a yoke of slavery" (Galatians 5:1). "But Peter and the apostles answered, 'We must obey God rather than men'" (Acts 5:29).

Meanwhile, there are those who have heard the biblical call to stand firm and obey the Lord, yet they have chosen to reject it.

> "Thus says the Lord:
> 'Stand by the roads, and look,
>   and ask for the ancient paths,
>   where the good way is; and walk in it, and find rest for
> your souls.'
> But they said, 'We will not walk in it.'" (Jeremiah 6:16)

The watchman described in Ezekiel 33 warns us against failing to speak when we see wrong. Who is to be a watchman in our time? Verses 2–4 say,

> Son of man, speak to your people and say to them, 'If I bring the sword upon a land, and the people of the land take a man from among them, and make him their watchman, and if he sees the sword coming upon the land and blows the trumpet and warns the people, then if anyone who hears the sound of the trumpet does not take

warning, and the sword comes and takes him away, his blood shall be upon his own head.'

Our duty, out of love, is to sound the alarm and warn the people. Love does not give us a license to disobey the clear righteousness set out by the Word of God. Instead, love speaks truth and warns people when danger is coming to a head. And if we love those who have been deceived into thinking they are believers in Christ, even as they live sinfully, then in love, we must speak truth to them and warn them against their sin.

As part of our boldness, we are called to be salt and light. What does that look like practically? How can we be the metaphorical salt and light if we aren't bold enough to stand firm on a daily basis?

We're told in Luke 8:16, "No one after lighting a lamp covers it with a jar or puts it under a bed, but puts it on a stand, so that those who enter may see the light." If we are going to be salt and light, we can't cover the truth. We have to demonstrate it. It's not comfortable. In fact, it can be a great challenge. But that's what we're called to.

We cannot be salt and light if we are ashamed of the gospel. In Romans 1:16, Paul says," For I am not ashamed of the gospel, for it is the power of God for salvation to everyone who believes, to the Jew first and also to the Greek."

If anything prevents us from demonstrating boldness, it is shame. But if we aren't ashamed of something, we can easily be bold. We can easily speak out or stand firm for something when we overcome any embarrassment or discomfort. It doesn't mean it will be comfortable; it just means we are choosing boldness because our hope and our boast is in Christ.

In former times, shame was still considered positive when it came to behaviors deemed immoral. It was shameful to do any of the following: have sex outside of marriage, steal, engage in homosexual relationships, and mistreat others. But in our current culture, the shame of evil has dissipated while the shame of weak Christians in their faith has increased.

When weak, professing Christians are no longer bold and those who indulge in evil are no longer ashamed, we see the balance of boldness shifting to the side of those who would gladly celebrate their sin. We see many videos of people unashamedly steal hundreds of dollars from stores as the police or clerks do nothing about it. The thieves are laughing and taking their time. Their attitude and their videos reflect a quiet confidence in their sin.

It's devastating to see this swing in accepted morality, but the Bible warned us a day would come when we call good evil and evil good. "Woe to those who call evil good and good evil, who put darkness for light and light for darkness, who put bitter for sweet and sweet for bitter!" (Isaiah 5:20). We are seeing a similar swing in the shame of sin being bold and the boldness of righteousness growing ashamed. This is a disturbing trend.

But how can we fight against it? Matthew 10:16 gives us some guidance when Jesus says, "Behold, I am sending you out as sheep in the midst of wolves, so be wise as serpents and innocent as doves." For those who have seen a pack of wolves against any prey, the message is clear. As we are the sheep of His hand, the message should pierce us. To be wise as serpents is to be bold, and to be innocent as doves is to use our boldness without belligerence.

Even before those who hate us, we can go before the Lord. We saw how Daniel responded to unjust laws, still praying boldly and without hiding. In Psalm 23:5, it says, "You prepare a table before me in the presence of my enemies; you anoint my head with oil; my cup overflows."

Romans 12:1–2 paints an ever clearer picture for us in saying, "I appeal to you therefore, brothers, by the mercies of God, to present your bodies as *a living sacrifice*, holy and acceptable to God, which is your spiritual worship. Do not be conformed to this world, but be transformed by the renewal of your mind, that by testing you may discern what is the will of God, what is good and acceptable and perfect" (emphasis added). The first verse clearly states that our bodies belong to God and God alone. If we are living sacrifices, that means we are wholly dedicated to him and there is no need for shame. We should always be ready to boldly stand firm, no matter the cost.

In the second verse, we are urged not to conform to the culture of the world. Our minds should continually be fixed on Christ. This is the very antithesis of the progressive church. And if we are standing firm against culture and lies, we have to stand against those who try to twist the Bible for their own means as well. The danger of these lies is impossible to overstate, so we must place our lives and our boldness in the hands of God. There is no way we can live a life in cooperation with both verses of Romans 12:1–2 without boldness.

Jesus prays in light of this, "I do not ask that you take them out of the world, but that you keep them from the evil one" (John 17:15). He specifically asks God not to just grab his people and run but that we would be able to stand firm here, where we are. It is a prayer for us to be strong, despite culture and despite the evils of this present age.

We are called to be ambassadors. We may not yet live in heaven with our King, but we are His representatives here on earth for as long as we live. That is our duty and should be our goal.

Can you imagine an ambassador who didn't speak out on behalf of their country or their country's interests? If an American ambassador went to Iran and just smiled and said, "Sure, take what you want," people would be horrified. So how can we expect to be ambassadors who don't speak out on behalf of Christ?

James Chalmers said, "I am immortal until my work for the Lord is done on Earth." Truly, as long as God has a purpose for us here, we will be here. And His great purpose is that we should stand firm and declare his name.

What Do They Want?

Sometimes we find ourselves looking at the other side of our culture and wonder what they even want. Why are they trying so hard to push some of the most absurd wickedness? What benefit could they possibly find in a society of children who identify as cats? What pleasure do they find in mocking the crucifixion at a baseball game or the Last Supper at the Olympics?[31]

Scientifically, you have to test that something is true in order to prove that the opposite is untrue. So if the Bible is saying we need to be bold, then let's look at what evil is saying. Evil tells us we need to be silent. So we must ask why evil wants us to be silent *and* why God

---

[31] David K. Li, "MLB players say drag troupe invited to Dodgers' Pride Night mocks Christianity," NBC News, May 31, 2023, https://www.nbcnews.com/nbc-out/out-news/mlb-players-say-drag-troupe-invited-dodgers-pride-night-mocks-christia-rcna87013; Matias Grez and Chris Liakos, "Organizers apologize after church groups criticize alleged 'Last Supper' parody during opening ceremony," CNN, July 29, 2024, https://www.cnn.com/2024/07/29/sport/last-supper-paris-olympic-opening-ceremony-spt-intl.

asks us to be bold.

For example, evil tells us to allow a child to be an over-sexualized cat and not to speak out against this as it's unloving to do so. In addition, some states are passing laws preventing parents from getting involved in their own child's life-changing situation, such as receiving gender-affirming care for a sex change.[32]

Of course, a truly loving parent would not allow their child to be so deceived and would speak truth to them out of the darkness of such deception, trusting the Holy Spirit to do his work in his time. But when the world tries so hard to convince others that Christians are hateful for their stance against sin, we have to stand firm even when it's uncomfortable.

Beyond attempting to silence us, they will ridicule us. They will mock us. They will look for ways to punish us. Culture may call us names or gaslight us, convincing others we are the problem. Anyone who has a belief in biblical morality will be called a White Christian Nationalist, regardless of their race or stance on theocracy.

And when we come to a point as Isabel Vaughn-Spruce in the UK did where we cannot even stand outside an abortion facility and silently pray without being arrested, we know the days for boldness have arrived.

An article in the *Guardian Magazine*, a beacon of liberalism, has said that in order to advocate atheism and to keep prayer out of schools, "They find abolishment significantly reduced religiousness, both in private (less praying) and public (church attendance)."[33] This suggests the idea that a lack of belief in faith does not lead to a demoralization of culture. To be frank, we have seen significant evidence to the contrary.

I consider my own children's experiences in school. My daughter's first day of homework at the start of the school year was to prove that there is no Creator. She was also told never to see a

---

[32] Ed Komenda, "Transgender minors protected from estranged parents under Washington law," PBS News, May 9, 2023, https://www.pbs.org/newshour/politics/transgender-minors-protected-from-estranged-parents-under-washington-law.

[33] Torstench Bell, "Ending religion lessons in schools leads to overall decline in belief but not morals," January 16, 2022, *The Guardian*, https://www.theguardian.com/commentisfree/2022/jan/16/ending-religion-lessons-in-schols-leads-to-overall-decline-in-belief-not-morals.

doctor who doesn't believe in evolution as such a person would not be trustworthy in their career.

My son has been told in school that we live in a post-truth world. The student newspaper at his school also affirms God as part of the LGBTQ community. Critical race theory was even taught there in chapel.

But why should any of this surprise us? In 2020, churches were shut down as "super spreaders." Meanwhile, strip clubs, casinos, and abortion clinics remained open.

And this is where we are. This is our society. This is our culture.

To my fellow believers in Christ who support biblical truths, this is not the time to merely get political, and it is not the time to be obnoxiously belligerent. Not only does the Bible require that we speak out, but we ought to see evil trying to silence us as further proof that we need to be bold.

This is the time to be bold!

CHAPTER 2

Obstacles to Being Bold

As we've seen, it's easy enough to see the value in being bold. It's another story to actually step out boldly when we're aware of the consequences. At times, even the boldest person is not bold at all.

Moses was a bold youth. In his indiscretion, he lashed out and killed an Egyptian whom he saw beating a Hebrew slave. "One day, when Moses had grown up, he went out to his people and looked on their burdens, and he saw an Egyptian beating a Hebrew, one of his people. He looked this way and that, and seeing no one, he struck down the Egyptian and hid him in the sand" (Exodus 2:11–12). This act of boldness was born out of a need for justice. Apparently, he acted based on his feelings, not based on God's power of boldness He gives us; however, we don't know enough about the circumstance to understand whether or not death was the justifiable response. But in this scene in Moses's life, we see that he was willing to be bold and stand when he saw a wicked incident that called for justice.

Later, we see Moses's boldness in himself transition to a God-given boldness, and he was able to stand up to Pharaoh. It took courage and strength to stand against the ruler of the most powerful nation at that time. Even after leading God's people to freedom, Moses had to stand up against his own Hebrew people multiple times during their trek through the desert and wilderness to lead them to the promised land. He constantly settled their complaints and called out their ingratitude when they came against him and lived like other nations, even sinking to creating idols. Moses boldly took a stand and handled the situations when they needed to be addressed.

Yet as easy as it is to look to the boldness of Moses, we can't forget he was just a regular man, and he had the same response any of us might have if we were told to stand before a world leader and make demands that would overturn their economy and culture.

When God called Moses to lead his people out of Egypt, Moses initially said no. He lost his desire to be bold as he had when he killed the Egyptian. He made up numerous excuses as to why he couldn't lead the Israelites as explained throughout Exodus 3–4. The Israelites wouldn't believe him, he insisted. He didn't think they'd accept him as a leader. He wasn't a strong speaker. So God gave him a speaker. He gave Moses signs to prove God's power and that God sent Moses to them. He struck down every argument Moses tried to raise. And ultimately, Moses found his boldness through God, even in these challenges.

History gives us many examples of other bold men and women, but they failed to act when they should have. Their regret led them to make significant changes and ultimately do great things. These people didn't just fail in their early attempts but failed to act at all. Most of us can probably relate to that. We all have times in our lives when we regret our inaction.

Biblically, we can also look to the apostle Peter. When he was challenged by the woman before Jesus's crucifixion, he denied Jesus three times, just as Jesus said he would. Hours before, he cut off the ear of one of the guards at the arrest of Jesus, but then this boldness disappeared. But between that regret and his passion for the gospel, Peter received the Holy Spirit, which transformed his boldness so he could lead the foundation of the church.

We can also look at the Lutheran Pastor, Martin Niemöller, whose famous quote resounds in so many situations when people face injustice.

> First they came for the socialists, and I did not speak out—because I was not a socialist.
> Then they came for the trade unionists, and I did not speak out—because I was not a trade unionist.

Then they came for the Jews, and I did not speak out—because I was not a Jew. Then they came for me—and there was no one left to speak for me.[34]

Niemöller said that early on, he was complicit in Nazism, even voting for the Nazi party in 1933. His first wake-up call was seeing how the party pushed themselves into church policy and later, he realized just how wicked they were. Once he decided to speak out, Niemöller ended up in prison for eight years.[35]

Malcolm X is another secular example of this inaction leading to regret and, ultimately, big steps to rectify the matter. People were speaking out against Elijah Muhammad, but Malcolm X initially defended him. When he recognized Muhammad's adultery and cover-up of affairs with multiple secretaries, Malcolm X finally stepped out. He traveled to Mecca and separated himself from Muhammad, which ultimately led to Malcolm X's death.[36]

Imagine what he went through. He had to speak out against the person he credited with saving his life—speaking out despite losing friends, his home, and his reputation. But he remained bold. Although Malcolm X was doing this for the Koran, Jesus asks us to carry our cross daily and prepares His followers to be persecuted.

Even as I write these words about proclaiming the importance of boldness, I consider the moments when I should have acted with more boldness than I did, even in the last week. It's certainly not limited to this week but throughout my past when I didn't respond as I should have. In fact, I'm sure that when I read through this again later, I'll say the same thing about that week. It's part of our human nature, and none of us is immune.

Our reality is that we are certainly no better than Moses. We all make excuses to stop ourselves from being bold. A mother may hesitate to speak up against an immoral school decision because she doesn't want to draw the attention of a corrupt local government who may target her or even her children. It's a fairly legitimate reason

---

[34] "Martin Niemöller: 'First they came for...,'" Holocaust Encyclopedia, accessed May 16, 2025, https://encyclopedia.ushmm.org/content/en/article/martin-niemoeller-first-they-came-for-the-socialists.

[35] Ibid.

[36] "Malcolm X," *Britannica*, last updated May 15, 2025, https://www.britannica.com/biography/Malcolm-X.

when she considers her responsibility to protect and be present with her children. This is why so many parents are becoming helicopter parents or bulldozer parents, definitions unheard of thirty years ago, because she would be putting them at risk of being unpopular or ridiculed as well, and that would be unbearable.

Likewise, a husband may keep his mouth shut at work, even referring to a coworker by dishonest pronouns because his duty as a husband and father is to provide for his family, and he can't risk losing his job. The Bible is clear about a man's duty to provide, so he could justify his decision as that sort of boldness and the consequences of it could contradict his calling as a husband and father.

With legitimate reasons, we can easily say we're just choosing between two different options of obedience. We aren't being silly like Moses and just blaming our fear on public speaking or whatever his speech issues may have been. We're staying quiet because we are protecting our family and standing firm in our duties. But is it really as simple as that?

We face these challenges in today's society, and in these times, we have to lean into God and his Word to discern the right action.

But even in less extreme examples, we truly can't be bold every single moment. As Christians, however, we should be careful with what we are bold about in the world. In matters of faith, our lack of boldness should be minimal. When these matters impact our faith, the church, or anything that could prevent us from doing God's work, we simply have to make the right decision. We have to be bold. Anything less is shame.

If we lack boldness, we must distinguish between moments of fear and strongholds of fear. What is a moment of lacking boldness? What is a stronghold?

For example, I recently had an opportunity to pray for a total stranger. He was suffering under the burden of cancer, and I could have prayed over him and for his healing. But I hesitated. I lost the opportunity. That moment could have made a difference for him, but I lost the moment due to my lack of boldness. It's still on my mind, and boldness would have been the best option. I hope this leads me to a different decision when I have another opportunity.

A stronghold is different. If I didn't pray for him or ever pray for anyone else, and I did this regularly and always made excuses and continued to refuse to honor the still, small voice, that would be a stronghold. If I chose to allow people to make fun of Christians who live out their faith, it would be a stronghold. If I lived in fear of being excluded because of my own faith, this would be a stronghold. Truly, we can't allow ourselves to constantly live in fear of boldness, or we aren't losing moments, we are losing opportunities to lean on Christ for his boldness.

Paul urges us to tear down these strongholds in 2 Corinthians 10:3–4: "For though we walk in the flesh, we are not waging war according to the flesh. For the weapons of our warfare are not of the flesh but have divine power to destroy strongholds." It couldn't be any clearer that we need to tear down the strongholds preventing us from standing firm.

Let's review what an actual stronghold was in biblical times. A stronghold was a large fortress. The metaphor Paul is using would be a fortress resistant to the truth.[37] We may face many strongholds in our lives: addictions, greed, or our own pride. But whatever other strongholds we need to overcome, the one we're dealing with here is the stronghold of excuses.

According to the *Merriam-Webster Dictionary*, the word *excuse* means to make apology for; to try to remove blame from."[38] An excuse actually means just what the word says. We think our behavior is excused or justified. We think there's a reason for it, just like the mother protecting her child from corruption or the father protecting his job so he can provide.

If I were to kill someone in self-defense, I would think my action was excused because it was the only choice to save my life. I had no other recourse to stop the attacker. However, if I were to use the excuse that I wasn't bold because I didn't want to be made fun of, would it be justified? Or would I believe standing up for God's truth is excused in the face of ridicule? How well do you think that excuse will work when you are face to face with Christ?

Clearly, there is a division between the two. If we seek to justify ourselves in the most important matters, we can justify ourselves in any circumstance. Returning to the idea of the progressive church,

---

[37] "Stronghold," Bible Hub, accessed May 16, 2025,
https://biblehub.com/topical/s/stronghold.htm.
[38] *Merriam-Webster Dictionary*, "excuse," accessed May 16, 2025,
https://www.merriam-webster.com/dictionary/excuse.

how many people do we know who we used to think were solid in their faith only to now see them justifying sin because it's too hard to stand firm against it? We absolutely must not sink to that same position.

If we are going to tear down the strongholds we face, we must look at the common obstacles we build. What do we use as our excuse to not be bold? How can we focus on becoming bolder and growing into the people who God intended us to be? How do we let go of strongholds and instead strengthen our firm foundations?

This is precisely what we will address in the coming pages. The following chapters will reflect on different excuses I've heard when people do try to explain their weak behavior. We'll look more at the frequent excuse that they're simply not bold like others. And we'll consider what happens when you start to question those people and the real reasons surface.

I challenge you, as you read each chapter, to think about how this applies to you. Ask yourself the hard questions:

- Do I struggle with this same obstacle?
- Do I even want to fix it?
- What steps will I take each week to fix this lack of boldness in my life?

This is a process. We can't take a bus heading east at sixty miles per hour and immediately turn it west. The bus will flip over. We have to slow the bus down, make the turn, and then speed up. We're seeking boldness, not belligerence. This takes time, focus, and a true desire to lean into Christ as your strength.

For Reflection

1. Reflect on a time when you felt a strong calling to act boldly but hesitated. What were the reasons behind your hesitation, and how can understanding these reasons help you overcome similar obstacles in the future?

2. Consider your own life. Do any strongholds, such as fear, pride, or excuses, consistently prevent you from being bold in your faith? How do these strongholds manifest in your daily decisions? What steps can you take to confront them?

3. Moses initially resisted God's call by making excuses about his leadership abilities and the Israelites' acceptance. What parallels can you draw between Moses's hesitations and your own excuses for not stepping out in boldness?

4. In what areas of your life do you feel called to be bolder in your faith? What specific steps can you take to strengthen your faith and overcome any hesitation in those areas?

5. As you read the following chapters, consider practical steps you can implement this week to start overcoming your own obstacles to boldness. Consider setting specific goals or actions that will help you practice and develop greater boldness. How can you intentionally practice boldness this week?

6. How will you measure your progress in becoming bolder over time? What indicators will show you that you are moving from moments of hesitation to consistently acting boldly in your faith?

CHAPTER THREE

Lack of Comfort

Comfort is one of the greatest things we seek, especially in modern times. So much of progress since the Industrial Revolution has been an effort to bring comfort, ease, and relief from the hardships faced by past generations. Comfort has become an idol in so much of the world, and in many ways, it has become more elusive than ever as anxiety rises, and in the US, at least, it seems as though you're not successful if you're not stressed.

But we have come to master certain areas of comfort. And I do believe the biggest obstacle we have when it comes to being bold is the fear of not being comfortable.

We get comfortable in the life we have. We don't want to lose that life. No matter the stress or the problems, at least we know our routine and know what to expect. We're comfortable. A couple of the biggest areas of our comfort are in our relationships and our finances.

We get comfortable in our relationships and desperately don't want to lose them. We fear what might happen if we lose the respect or trust of someone because we stand up for something different. We may have family members who would be angry if we told them they did something wrong. It would be deeply uncomfortable to lose a friend group that stopped inviting you to parties or nights out because you chose to stop drinking. Even if you didn't judge them or say anything about their drinking, they might feel guilty or not want to be seen with you anymore. Often when people want to be sober, their families won't invite them to family reunions or even a small cookout. If that family believes their sobriety is because the person got saved, they assume they will be judged. They will criticize their sobriety, and even though the newly sober person may be making a better choice for themselves, the fear of losing their family may be enough so that they fall off the wagon again.

In my business, I had a manager who worked for me for many years. He was a great employee, but he struggled when we transitioned to a faith-forward company. He was asked if this changed for him. He responded by saying we did good things before and we do good things now. But the difference between then and now is that now we were telling people the reasons why we were doing those things.

Therefore, he thought there was no real change. He went along with all the new policies and even reminded other employees not to use bad language. "We are a Christian company now. We don't cuss anymore." He enforced and held our company's new moral standards. However, he was still struggling.

One day, he was having a particularly hard day. He was trying to manage his workload while also balancing his personal life. In my office, he broke down. I thought this was an opportunity to share the gospel, so I did. Unfortunately, he rejected what I said. Several weeks later, he gave his notice and left our company.

I thought about it for a while, wondering what I should have done differently.

- Maybe it was not the right time.
- Maybe I was too direct
- Maybe I misread the situation.
- Maybe I was coming across too strong.
- Maybe . . . maybe . . . maybe . . .

Shortly thereafter, I was speaking with a friend about Muslims and how, when they turn to Christ, they lose friends and family. Their entire social circle and networks are gone. This happens to many Muslims around the world. They struggle if they turn away from their family's religion in order to follow Jesus. They risk losing their entire family and being rejected by those they know and are closest to. However, sometimes they have an even greater risk, even of losing their lives. Sometimes death by a family member is the consequence of this decision.

The same is often true for atheists and secularists in our country. If this employee had made the decision to accept and follow Christ, he would be making huge sacrifices. He would lose the woman he loved, who was a very liberal, anti-Christian, live-in girlfriend. He would lose their entire friend group of fake, upper-crust, intellectual Green Party enthusiasts. And these relationships were his main source of comfort.

It's no wonder he was unwilling to let go of them if he didn't know how much greater the comfort of knowing Christ would be. He was primed to share the gospel with, but he couldn't give up the things he had in this world.

Even Jesus talks about the struggle of battling the cares of the world. In the parable of the sower, Jesus talks about what happens when the seed, the gospel, falls among the thorns. "The seed falling among the thorns refers to someone who hears the word, but the worries of this life and the deceitfulness of wealth choke the word, making it unfruitful" (Matthew 13:22). These are just a few examples of how we can lose our comfort if we make the decision to accept Christ.

But these consequences are also true for many Christians who gave their lives to Jesus early on—before slowly becoming friends with the world. Many people were raised in the standard American evangelical church culture, getting baptized at a young age, going to youth group, and somewhat regularly reading their Bibles.

But then, they faced the appeals of friendships outside of their church. The popular kids may notice them or they find a chance to gain acceptance from the people they admire most. The pressure becomes too much, and they may tone down their religious activity in order to remove any barriers between them and those people.

In college, they might join a fraternity or sorority. The pleasures of drugs, alcohol, and sex are prevalent. The relationships they've developed will encourage these temptations, easing the burden of guilt they may have felt once upon a time.

And then, they transition into adulthood. Their friendships really don't change that much. Their college sweetheart is now their spouse. They are each living a safe life. They know what to expect of one another. They know what to expect of their friend community.

And if the draw of their youthful faith returns, it would be devastating. To speak out now against any aspects of the lifestyle they all led would hurt. Those friendships would crack with the friends wondering why they are being so vocal or obnoxious. They wouldn't understand. The spouse might not be ready for such a shift and might not understand their change.

You may fear that people will say, "I remember you when . . ." Everything might change, and that would be extremely painful.

When I got saved and I would speak boldly about Christ, I had one of two responses:

- I was left out
- I was warned that my boldness would push people away from Christ.

No one wants to be left out, and no one wants to push people away from Christ even as they try to draw others to him. In that sense, these arguments can be very convincing.

The fear of missing out (FOMO) is deeply embedded in our culture. It ranges from little things like a woman wanting the pretty purse she sees on Instagram or a man wondering if a single property investment could lead him to a four-hour workweek like he heard on a podcast. But mostly, this FOMO idea refers to not wanting to be left out of specific activities or relationships.

We can change our perspective, however. We don't have to look at it this way at all. Instead of thinking you've been left out due to your faith, why not ask if you were really meant to be there in the first place? If God wanted you there, then you would be there. If he wanted you at that party, your friends would have invited you. If he wanted you to be included, you would be.

However, what I found was that the more I was left out, the more I didn't want to be there anyway. I stopped desiring to be in those situations and even around those people. I didn't push them away, but I wasn't desperate to be seen or heard anymore.

Bold people don't push others away from Christ. If they did, the early church would never have gained any momentum, and it would certainly have stalled ever since. Jesus Christ himself could not have been successful, given his own boldness.

A key element of faith, salvation, and our role in this world is to realize the most important point of all. Who is in charge of salvation? It is the work of Christ through the Holy Spirit to bring us to God. That means it is not our personal job to bring people to God. We aren't responsible for their conversion.

Our job is to share the gospel openly and willingly. We trust the Holy Spirit to do the work of conversion. We will not be 100 percent successful in seeing the Holy Spirit work in the lives of those we share the gospel with. Some will reject Him. Jesus Himself lost followers. "After this many of his disciples turned back and no longer walked with him" (John 6:66).

But if we are operating in fear and use the excuse that it's not our job to save people and the Holy Spirit will do it without us, we have to ask ourselves the following questions:

- How does being weak convince people to follow Christ?
- We never know how God will use our boldness, but how can anything good come out of our weakness?
- How can you share the gospel by being silent? If your relationships are holding you back from being bold, you can't use this excuse. You can't push the responsibility of the work on the Holy Spirit when, in reality, you are called to boldness.

Why would God call us to be bold if it actually pushed others away and kept them from approaching him? Would he really be cruel enough to call us to something designed to fail and use our obedience as an excuse to send others to hell? That makes no sense.

I've lost a lot of friends. I can only think of one friend in my life from before I was saved who still invites me to do anything. Am I lonely now? Do I not have a social life? No. God has blessed me with different friends, friends who care about me deeply and wholly. I can do life with them and be myself with them. These people are actually different. The fact is, God has blessed me with more people in my life that I can rely on for help than I've ever had before.

I am fortunate that, despite having lost friends I valued, I've been given so much more through the relationships I now enjoy.

Yet, it isn't only friends that people fear losing. A much greater risk is the loss of family. That threat can break someone's willingness to make the hard choice of boldness. Jesus tells us that we will lose family. We see this clear warning in Scripture and need to understand it if we're going to accept the consequences of this life. But we are also gaining a new family.

In living for Christ and in our boldness, we are becoming children of God. Our family may not look the same, but we will spend eternity with these brothers and sisters. They understand what it actually means to love sacrificially and to share the growth and intimacy of life in Christ.

If you truly care that much about your family, wouldn't you want to spend eternity with them? And if you don't want to lose the earthly family you're so close to, what more reason to boldly share the gospel with them so that they will join you in that eternity?

Another Comfort

Friends and family are deeply important to us, but we need to look at and touch on another important source of comfort. We may not initially realize our attachment to this comfort, but we have to recognize it if we're going to live the way we should: the comfort of our finances. We are comfortable in our financial situation. Does this mean we are secure and never worry about money? Not at all. Comfort in our finances doesn't necessarily mean we're content with our situation or that we aren't struggling. But it does mean we know, generally, what we need and how much we will get.

How can boldness in Christ put this at risk? We've already touched on it a little bit, but we certainly are at risk when we step out and choose to be vocal. Just as Jaelene Daniels and Paige Casey lost their careers due to their boldness, we wonder if boldness will cost us our own jobs. Would you lose your job if you don't use a person's preferred pronoun? Would you lose your job if you spoke out against a company ad featuring a lifestyle you disagree with? Would you lose a sale if you didn't cater to a specific type of customer or a need they might have? We see these examples in culture all the time when it comes to sexuality and abortion, but they go beyond that. The world is accepting all kinds of attitudes and behaviors.

Some have job applications rejected because they refuse to work on Sundays. Professors and teachers have also faced criticism or disciplinary review when they resist grading or teaching practices they feel violate their conscience—for example, being pressured to consider identity characteristics in ways they believe compromise academic fairness or personal conviction.

For example, Dr. Nicholas Meriwether, a professor at Shawnee State University, was disciplined for refusing to use a student's preferred pronouns. He argued this conflicted with his Christian beliefs and ultimately prevailed in court, receiving a settlement for violation of his First Amendment rights.39

We can absolutely pay a price due to bold refusal to submit to certain workplace policies that conflict with our beliefs. Our convictions can cost us a job, a promotion, or even our reputation and future within that industry.

Until or unless our culture changes, these possibilities are a real threat. But changing our culture comes through this very boldness. And ultimately, we will lose our finances anyway, whether in this world or in eternity. The question is which we value more.

We have to trust God to see us through our financial concerns. He is the provider of all we have anyway. He's the One who opened the door for the job we have, so we can trust our future in His hands for whatever happens next and whatever consequences we may face for our boldness. That doesn't mean an immediate reward. It may be miserably hard for a time. But he is the source, and we can trust His sovereignty through it all (Psalm 27).

Even if all this weren't the case, the Word of God is very clear. If we make our finances an idol and center our decisions about boldness around them, then we will lose them. But we will also lose him.

---

39 *"Dr. Nicholas Meriwether's Story,"* Alliance Defending Freedom, February 28, 2023, https://adflegal.org/article/dr-nicholas-meriwether-story.

For Reflection

1. Are you hesitant to make changes because you fear losing the comfort of your current routine? Are you holding onto comfort at the expense of growth? How can you step out of your comfort zone to embrace the changes that will bring spiritual growth and fulfillment?

2. Do you avoid standing up for your beliefs or values to maintain harmony in relationships? How can you stand firm in your faith while maintaining loving and respectful relationships with others?

3. Are you unwilling to pursue opportunities or make decisions that could potentially disrupt your financial stability? What risks are you unwilling to take for the sake of living out your values or calling?

4. Do you feel anxious or stressed when faced with the possibility of losing personal relationships or social status? How can you prioritize God's call over the fear of social repercussions?

5. Have you noticed you am more concerned about how others perceive you than about your own principles or faith? How can you focus more on living according to your values than on how others view you?

6. Are you struggling to balance your personal life with your professional or spiritual commitments, feeling overwhelmed by the potential loss of comfort? How can you navigate this tension while maintaining boldness in your priorities?

7. Do you experience difficulty making decisions that involve potential sacrifice, even when those decisions align with my core values or faith? How can you better align your choices with your core values, even when it requires sacrifice?

8. Are you resistant to expressing your true self or beliefs in social or professional settings to avoid potential backlash? How can you be more authentic in sharing your beliefs while navigating

challenging environments?

9. Do you feel more secure in your comfort zone, even if it means compromising your values or missing out on potential growth opportunities? How can you challenge yourself to step out of your comfort zone and pursue opportunities that align with your faith?

10. Are you worried about the long-term impact of losing your current level of comfort, which could affect your overall well-being and happiness? How can you trust God with the long-term impact of your choices and step forward in boldness, even when the future feels uncertain?

CHAPTER FOUR

Lack of Commitment

When we look at what is standing in the way of boldness, we also have to consider our own lack of commitment. This isn't pleasant to think about as we all want to believe we're doing everything we can to serve the Lord and to uphold righteousness, but we do need to acknowledge the limitations of our own commitment and our determination to obey.

Sometimes our lack of boldness is couched in that comfort or fear of losing relationships, but often, this lack of commitment is the real root of the issue. We need to look at what it means to have true commitment. Is commitment part of our nature or is it a choice? And when we don't respond with the level of commitment we have been called to, is it because we don't truly care about the commitment? Or are we just plain lazy?

Maybe we are verbally committed to defending our faith, but when it comes to regular reading of Scripture, it's not a priority. We aren't motivated. How, then, can we defend our faith as presented in the Bible if we aren't reading it?

Or maybe we watch a lot of news and are very happy and bold in arguing morality from a political perspective. But Sundays are a nice day to rest, and we struggle to get to church every week, so it's hard to argue morality from a theological perspective. And if you're debating with a progressive Christian who does attend church regularly, you're going to have to fight against some serious indoctrination.

Laziness and apathy will definitely prevent us from living in the way we are called to. And while this doesn't make you a bad person by any means, it's very important to acknowledge. There are a number of verses about laziness, but consider Proverbs 24:30–34:

> I passed by the field of a sluggard, by the vineyard of a man lacking sense, and behold, it was all overgrown with thorns; the ground was covered with nettles, and its stone wall was broken down. Then I saw and considered it; I looked and received instruction. A little sleep, a little slumber, a little folding of the hands to rest, and poverty will come upon you like a robber, and want like an armed man.

If a man has a vineyard and he's lazy in how he cares for it, it falls apart and becomes overgrown by weeds, and he ultimately ends up poor. How much more does this happen in our spiritual lives when we become lazy? How can we stand up to culture when it's uncomfortable if our own hearts are overgrown with weeds and our foundations are broken down? So while laziness doesn't necessarily make us bad people, it does impact our ability to stand firm in the way the Bible has urged us to do.

We will always be passionate about certain causes and people and not about others. There's nothing wrong with this. We're different humans with different perspectives. Not every human can be passionately committed to every single cause. For example, my wife is passionate about certain causes while I am passionate about others. Her background and upbringing have led her to be passionate about health-related causes. Since her family was impacted by health-related circumstances growing up, these matter deeply to her. I, however, am more passionate about political causes or matters related to injustice. If you've read my previous books or know much about me, you may know I am passionate about marginalized people. I am passionate when I see people being bullied by larger groups, businesses, government, etc. Therefore, my experiences have led me to take a stand when I see these issues.

My causes aren't better than hers, but rather, I feel strongly about certain issues due to my life experiences. Her life experiences have caused her to feel passionate about other issues. My wife agrees that my causes and charities are valuable and important. I agree that her causes and charities are valuable and important.

Different backgrounds can cause us to see people differently as well. Of course, how we see people impacts more than just our different opinions on charities and are the result of more than just our upbringings. Some people out there may rub me the wrong way as soon as I meet them. It's not always easy to share Jesus with these people when I really want to share my fist in their face. But we're here to talk about boldness, not the satisfying belligerence that would come of that sort of violence!

In other scenarios, we have to accept the fact that sometimes we lack the boldness because we do not care. We may not care about a specific person, or we may just not care about a moment or opportunity. This doesn't make you a bad person, but we need to consider this when we are not bold so we don't allow this weakness or obstacle to spread to other parts of our lives.

Oftentimes, people use these sorts of excuses, just saying they aren't bold enough. But this is not a matter of not being bold. In reality, it is a problem stemming from a lack of commitment. If you are not committed to doing the work of Christ, this needs to be addressed. We can't depend on excuses, and we can't just lean on a sigh and a half-hearted vow to do better next time.

I have a business card I occasionally hand to employees. It says, "There are only two options: 1. Make progress. 2. Make excuses. You cannot do both."

Can you imagine telling your boss, "I didn't make any sales today because I just didn't feel like it?" That likely wouldn't go over well in the workplace. And if you care at all about your job, it's inadvisable to say that. And yet that's what we do every day when we don't engage boldly in the opportunities the Lord puts before us. When you're not bold due to a lack of commitment to the ministry of Jesus, your Lord, then you are telling him, "I just didn't feel like it."

More than Us

Beyond looking at our own souls, the Bible also teaches us to care about the salvation of others. After all, if our duty on earth is to be ambassadors of Christ as a part of our worship, we need to care about the eternal lives of those around us.

Scripture gives us abundant examples of this, but Paul makes it very plain when he shares his concerns about the Galatians. He had loved these people dearly and reached them with the gospel. And yet, despite having the free grace of Jesus, they were turning back to the ways of the Jews, putting themselves under the old covenant law. While the law is the antithesis of what we are seeing in our modern times, it displays the concern we ought to have for others who are not living within the freedom of the gospel.

> Formerly, when you did not know God, you were enslaved to those that by nature are not gods. But now that you have come to know God, or rather to be known by God, how can you turn back again to the weak and worthless elementary principles of the world, whose slaves you want to be once more? You observe days and months and seasons and years! I am afraid I may have labored over you in vain.
>
> Brothers, I entreat you, become as I am, for I also have become as you are. You did me no wrong. You know it was because of a bodily ailment that I preached the gospel to you at first, and though my condition was a trial to you, you did not scorn or despise me, but received me as an angel of God, as Christ Jesus. What then has become of your blessedness? For I testify to you that, if possible, you would have gouged out your eyes and given them to me. Have I then become your enemy by telling you the truth? They make much of you, but for no good purpose. They want to shut you out, that you may make much of them. It is always good to be made much of for a good purpose, and not only when I am present with you, my little children, for whom I am again in the anguish of childbirth until Christ is formed in you! I wish I could be present with you now and change my tone, for I am perplexed about you. (Galatians 4:8–20)

Examples like this should urge us to be honest with our friends who may have proclaimed Christianity in the past but are drifting into progressivism, using Jesus as a scapegoat for social justice and open sin. It is right that we should be perplexed about them.

Our approach must always be out of love for them and a true desire to see them reconciled to God and to truth, but just as Paul pointed out a rejection of the gospel in favor of the law, we need to be concerned about those who have rejected the gospel in favor of the world and its comforts.

But we shouldn't only care for those who claim to be Christians. The souls of those who have never received Jesus or are blatantly living a life in contradiction to truth should also matter to us.

The Great Commission in Matthew 28:18–20 says, "And Jesus came and said to them, 'All authority in heaven and on earth has been given to me. Go therefore and make disciples of all nations, baptizing them in the name of the Father and of the Son and of the Holy Spirit, teaching them to observe all that I have commanded you. And behold, I am with you always, to the end of the age.'" Jesus has commissioned us to go into the world as his witnesses, standing firm and discipling others. So many hearts are willing to hear, but we stumble because we face a few people who are so hard-hearted that we think it's hopeless.

Sharing the truth with others is simultaneously the simplest and the hardest thing in the world. It should be a natural part of us that exudes from our own boldness and passion for the goodness and mercy of God. And yet, our attempts to be sensitive to others for fear of the risk of losing those relationships or being rejected makes it difficult. We are dealing with other broken sinners, just as we have been (and continue to be but redeemed by the grace of God). The discomfort, however, should mean little to us.

In John 15:9–13, Jesus paints us another picture of himself as the vine bearing fruit.

> As the Father has loved me, so have I loved you. Abide in my love. If you keep my commandments, you will abide in my love, just as I have kept my Father's commandments and abide in his love. These things I have spoken to you, that my joy may be in you, and that your joy may be full.
>
> This is my commandment, that you love one another as I have loved you. Greater love has no one than this, that someone lay down his life for his friends.

These words demonstrate to us that He has sacrificed His own life out of His love for us. If we truly have love for our friends and family who don't know God or even the stranger with whom we unexpectedly find ourselves in conversation, we should be willing to lay down our lives.

Yes, in many places in the world and at many times throughout history, such a conversation really could lead to death. But these days, we are scarcely willing to experience the discomfort mentioned in the previous chapter. If we aren't committed to really knowing Christ and sharing him with others, we reject the love we are called to.

For Reflection

1. Am I consistently prioritizing my spiritual growth and practices, such as Bible study, prayer, and church attendance?

2. When I face opportunities to share my faith or stand up for my beliefs, do I find myself hesitant or making excuses?

3. Think about your involvement in your church community. Are you actively participating, or is there room for improvement in your engagement?

4. Reflect on situations where following your faith meant stepping out of your comfort zone. How did you handle those moments?

5. Evaluate how your personal interests and passions reflect your commitment to Christ. Are they aligned, or do they conflict at times?

6. Do you have actionable steps in place to grow in your faith? What are they, and how can you stay committed to them?

7. Consider areas where you may be spiritually apathetic or lazy. How can you address this and reignite your commitment to spiritual practices?_

8. How do I respond to challenges or setbacks in my faith journey? Do I persevere or give up easily?

9. Think about whether you have people in your life who hold you accountable for your spiritual growth. How can you seek out more support if needed?

10. Consider your concern for others' faith. How can you translate this concern into tangible actions, such as offering support or sharing the gospel?

CHAPTER FIVE

Lack of Convenience

Sometimes we need to be bold even when it is not convenient for us. Once, I was in Detroit speaking to a Christian business group. I had left my jacket at home, so I had to stop to buy one. I had been running a few minutes ahead of schedule, but now I was going to be late.

I hate being late. It really stresses me out. It is so bad that my wife and I have to take separate cars to church as I need to be there early, and she is on time or a few minutes late. We have to do this to eliminate any tension because I must be early. So imagine that I was the speaker for this group and I was going to be late on top of this.

I quickly googled a department store and found one in route, so I rushed there to make my purchase as fast as I possibly could. I found a jacket in my budget, but it wasn't in my size, so I asked if they had one in the back. They did not, but he brought me a jacket that was similar in color and style that was my size. I handed him my credit card and started cutting the tags off. I sprinted to my car and headed to the event.

After dinner, in my hotel room, I looked at my credit card slip and realized I paid more for this jacket than I have for any clothing item that I have ever bought. To this day, it is my most expensive article of clothing.

I tell this story as an example of our hurried nature and need for convenience. If I was rushing so quickly that I didn't even recognize what I had paid for the jacket, I may not have even noticed an opportunity to be bold. For all I know, I might have had an amazing opportunity right in front of my face to share the gospel, but in my hurry, I missed it. Maybe I passed someone on the street. Or maybe if I had looked at the price tag, I could have spoken to the employee about how I believe money is a gift from God to steward well. Who knows what I hurried past that day? And who knows what we pass almost any day when we are rushing around, trying to do what needs to be done?

Even if I had seen an opportunity to be bold (depending on the opportunity), I probably would not have taken the time to do it. I was in a hurry, and I knew I had to get to the event. Did I really want to take time to chat with the employee about the theology of finances? What else do we overlook on a daily basis because we have somewhere more important to be and something more important to do? We've looked at a few common excuses people give about why they are unwilling to be bold. But what about this matter of convenience and how it gets in the way?

Yes, a lot of these matters are idols in Western culture—especially comfort and convenience—but when it comes to our time and our energy, we tend to be very selfish. The idea of convenience can be extremely blinding when we're faced with certain situations, and we have to decide whether or not we will lay aside our own momentary convenience for the sake of boldness.

Many times, I've prayed for a person while running to an appointment, but I didn't bother communicating that I prayed for them. I invited God into the situation, but I lacked boldness because I felt I was too busy.

It's easy to say, "When XYZ happens, then I will be better. Then, I'll be bold enough." For example, one might say, "Once I stop smoking, then I will be bold, but I don't want people to think I'm a hypocrite." Or, "If someone asks me a question, then I will answer, but I want to wait for them to speak first." Our boldness might require a financial sacrifice, so we commit that we'll take that bold step once we get a raise at work.

Or it requires missing a couple of hours with our family because a neighbor is in distress, and we can be there for them and share the gospel, but it's been a tough week, and we just want to spend some time resting with our spouse. We tell ourselves we'll be there for the neighbor tomorrow because our workload will be lighter. But what if tomorrow comes, and it's still not convenient? What about all the other tasks we didn't finish yesterday because we needed to prioritize our family time?

We make these half-hearted commitments to ourselves, knowing that by the time the circumstances are perfect, we will probably have forgotten or it will be too late. It's easy to tell ourselves we will do something when the timing is right, but it really comes down to our need for convenience and our selfishness.

Many people have addressed the change in culture and how we have gone from a community focus to individualistic. This is hard to deny, and we can't pretend we're somehow above that. In truth, our expectations are extremely self-involved, and most Americans have main-character syndrome to an extent. Sometimes being bold means having the patience to sit through a conversation with someone, but even when you are patient, it is not always convenient to take the time to listen, especially when we are so self-involved.

What has caused this? A number of things. But when we break it down, we essentially live in a McDonald's restaurant. We hit a couple buttons, submit our order, and receive the food. It's instant gratification. All around us, we have this opportunity. Want a new car? Just go to the dealership. Don't have the money for it? Get a loan. Drive the car home.

Want a new t-shirt? Type it into Amazon, add it to your cart, choose your payment method of a credit or debit card (or get your very own Amazon credit card, and you'll get an eighty dollar gift card to apply to this order!), and pick same-day shipping. In a couple hours, open the door, grab the package, rip it open, and wear your new t-shirt to dinner that night.

We always want to click the next button and move on to the next step of our own plan for our own time and our own money in our own life. If it doesn't work right away or the way I wanted, we get uptight and upset. Should the Wi-Fi go down, call the company and yell at the person on the other side of the phone so that they fix the issue faster. Should an accident happen on the highway when you're almost to your destination, see if you can take a side road.

Convenience is like a drug. Nothing can stand in our way when we want a dopamine hit from getting something instantly. So if something might come between us and that convenience, of course, we will look for excuses to eliminate the problem.

Oftentimes, we feel so busy and overwhelmed with our own plans that we don't even seem to have the time to spend listening to God, much less having face-to-face conversations with others. It isn't always convenient to spend that time with God. I generally do this in the mornings, but when I oversleep or hit my snooze button one too many times, it's not convenient to devote that time like I'd planned.

Convenience has become an idol, stealing our time with God. We often view it as a temptation used by Satan, just as Satan tempted Jesus in the wilderness. In Luke 4:3, Satan tempts Jesus to turn stones into bread, offering the immediate convenience of food. Similarly, in Luke 4:5–7, Satan offers Jesus the kingdom immediately, tempting him with the convenience of instant gratification rather than waiting and enduring suffering.

> The devil said to him, "If you are the Son of God, command this stone to become bread." And Jesus answered him, "It is written, 'Man shall not live by bread alone.'" And the devil took him up and showed him all the kingdoms of the world in a moment of time, and said to him, "To you I will give all this authority and their glory, for it has been delivered to me, and I give it to whom I will. If you, then, will worship me, it will all be yours." (Luke 4:3–7)

Our desire for convenience has allowed us to delegate spiritual responsibilities. When something is inconvenient, we let others handle it. We rely on the praise team for worship, delegate our daily Bible reading to a pastor who summarizes God's Word for us, and leave prayer to small groups at church.

When my father was having surgery, our corporate chaplain came, spent time with him beforehand, and prayed over him. In contrast, my father's priest arrived late because that's when he preferred to talk with family members in the cafeteria. He asked if we could donate food to their church during a kitchen renovation and, as he was leaving, casually mentioned, "Oh yes, the women at church are praying for your father too." His actions and words indicated that he did not want to actively participate in prayer as it was not convenient. He seemed to want to avoid the hard work and take advantage of the opportunity to satisfy his need. This desire for convenience robbed him of the opportunity to spend time with God but also to show others the value of doing sol.

Convenience signifies we are not fully acknowledging God's holiness, righteousness, and worthiness of our praise. We prioritize a lifestyle of ease over reverence for the One who spoke the world into existence. By choosing convenience, we forego meaningful engagement and worship, opting instead for distractions like our favorite shows, which fit more conveniently into our schedules.

But spending time with God helps give you the boldness you need to really carry out his will and calling for you as an ambassador. It is part of the plan to become bold. We will discuss this later, but it's important to think about now.

Occasionally, I will block out specific times in my calendar, times for no other purpose than to be with God. It may be a hike or just time by myself, but it's a chance to sit still and listen and meditate on him alone. I don't have my phone or any distractions with me. I find it's exceedingly helpful to get away from the busyness and just be with him.

I once went to a monastery for a silent retreat for three days. This may not be within everyone's capability, but the chance to get away and focus solely on my relationship with God for three days was a balm for the busyness of daily life.

When we make time for God, we have much greater peace in our lives, which so many are lacking. If we look at our phones and see how much time we spend on social media or on the phone in general, we can easily see where our focus lies. We can see the dramatic difference between that and our time with God. It's hard to be bold if we aren't spending that time with him. He gives us strength and courage, but we don't have peace if we're distracted by the world.

We need to ask ourselves the hard question: What are we doing consistently that is more important than spending time with God?

For Reflection

1. Reflect on how much you prioritize convenience in your life. Do you avoid bold actions because they are inconvenient or uncomfortable?

2. Think about instances when timing held you back from acting boldly. How often do you wait for the perfect moment instead of stepping out in faith?

3. How do you react when an opportunity for boldness disrupts your personal plans or schedule?

4. Think about times when you delayed faith-related responsibilities due to inconvenience. What steps can you take to prioritize these tasks?

5. Do I find myself making excuses about timing or circumstances for why I can't engage in faith-related activities? Reflect on your excuses. Are you letting convenience hold you back from fulfilling your calling to be bold in your faith?

6. How do you respond when your routine or plans are disrupted by an opportunity to help or share your faith? Do you make the most of these moments, or do you find reasons to avoid them?

7. Reflect on how you balance activities that offer instant pleasure with those that nurture your spiritual life. Where can you adjust your priorities?

8. Think about your spiritual routines. Are you intentional about making time for God, even when it's inconvenient?

9. Reflect on how often you focus on inconvenience instead of the significance of your actions. How can you shift your mindset to prioritize boldness over convenience?_

10. Identify the distractions that keep you from prioritizing

time with God. How can you address these barriers and be more intentional in your spiritual practices?

CHAPTER SIX

Lack of Confidence

One of the biggest obstacles for people when it comes to a lack of boldness is probably a lack of confidence. Other excuses aside, people seem to struggle with their own ability to discuss the very issue they're faced with. This so often prevents them from actually stepping out in the way they know they should. So they have a strong, underlying reason to shy away from conflict.

They may not be lacking confidence in God, although they certainly could be. But usually, they lack confidence that they know the Bible in such a way that they can confidently address topics head on. Most of the time, these people aren't belligerent. Instead, they are in compromise—which is a whole other topic we've briefly touched on.

People are afraid that if they speak up about a controversial subject, they will be asked a challenging question. They might not know the answer. Then what? Wouldn't they just look foolish? And wouldn't that just make their argument seem weak? In a lot of cases, people can justify that it's better for them to stay quiet instead of risking exposing their own ignorance. But as I said, much of the time, this is the natural result of not knowing the Bible well.

This is a huge problem because the opposing side could memorize three random verses in the Bible, and then they expect you to know which three they picked. They then discredit you for not having an answer to refute their false biblical take.

For instance, it's a popular argument in the pro-life movement that the pro-choice perspective dehumanizes people (suggesting that the fetus is not yet fully human) in the same way that chattel slavery dehumanized people (its proponents once arguing that certain races of people are less than human). The pro-choice movement has, reciprocally, pointed out specific Scripture verses that appear to promote slavery or to encourage slaves to obedience.

Unless a Christian has confidence in their knowledge of Scripture and their ability to view the context of the Bible as a whole, this can be an extremely challenging trap.

We must live according to Hebrews 10:34–39 which says,

> For you had compassion on those in prison, and you joyfully accepted the plundering of your property, since you knew that you yourselves had a better possession and an abiding one. Therefore do not throw away your confidence, which has a great reward. For you have need of endurance, so that when you have done the will of God you may receive what is promised. For, 'Yet a little while, and the coming one will come and will not delay; but my righteous one shall live by faith, and if he shrinks back, my soul has no pleasure in him.' But we are not of those who shrink back and are destroyed, but of those who have faith and preserve their souls.

This is worth remembering as you read on and how it relates to future chapters, especially chapter 10, regarding compassion. But these verses also remind us just how important it is to not shrink back and be destroyed. Have confidence not in yourself but in the truth of the gospel. Have this confidence even when you find yourself cowered in the trap of those whose arguments you aren't entirely sure how to fight.

Beyond just our uncertainty or lacking answers in the heat of the moment, we see an additional problem. I'll use an analogy to address it. I am terrible with names. I see people, and then I forget their names when I see them in a different context. Then, I feel stupid when I should know their name and it gets awkward. Then, when I do see them in the proper context and should remember their name, my confidence in remembering names is so bad that I don't think I'm remembering correctly when I really do. I second guess myself even if I am certain of their name.

So what do I do? I change my approach and do not use their

name. Then people think I am rude, which is not my intent. I'm just trying to cover my embarrassment or discomfort because I'm not confident I have the right answer.

This type of situation happens with quite a few people. They may know the answer, but they aren't prepared for the onslaught of cynical questions that may come next. Therefore, they keep quiet, thinking it's the safest and best option.

In addition to the abortion debate, we constantly see other hot topics in culture today. A Christian may know that homosexuality and transgenderism are wrong and antithetical to what the Bible tells us about God's design for creation. Yet when confronted, they may be quiet about it. Or even worse, they may compromise so they don't aren't hit with an onslaught of questions or attacks. They don't want to lose the argument. Sometimes a Christian will know political arguments better than biblical ones, so they just stay quiet altogether.

To compound this problem, the other side will often try to take advantage of this lack of confidence. We can start to turn away from God's truth and let ourselves get comfortable so we don't have to live with the reality that we're lacking in confidence.

The biggest trap used to further break our confidence—and for us to start moving further away from God and become less bold—is the redefining of terms. Truthfully, this tactic is being used more and more frequently by Western society. Politically, we may cynically say it's right out of *1984*, but if we look at it from a historical and biblical perspective, it's far more sinister.

Time and time again, non-Christians, or very weak Christians, for that matter, tell me how to live out my faith. If my confidence is already shaken due to my lack of knowledge, I will just accept their position as true rather than try to fight on their home turf. Losing this battle would put me deeper into a pit of losing confidence.

With the redefinition of terms, we are not arguing two sides of the same coin; we are arguing the morality of two different concepts or ideas that happen to share one name. For example, two words that are constantly redefined in modern culture are *love* and *judging*. These are the primary ones I used to employ when I was not a Christian and would attack Christians, so I do understand that, these days, both these words have a new meaning. This new meaning may not be accurate, but it is considered culturally acceptable and more and more people are clinging to it for the sake of comfort.

If I change the definition of *love* to mean "approval" and the definition of *judgment* to mean "arrogance," then it is impossible to defend any faith—much less the Christian faith where these two words have a glorious depth necessary to our understanding of a holy God.

Most of Scripture is in Hebrew and Greek. While the Greek have four different words for *love*, the main idea of love we see in the Bible has to do with *agape*, sacrificial love, the kind of love Christ exhibited on the cross when he died as a ransom for us all.[40]

And, biblically, judgment is a righteous act. God uses judgment to separate the holy from the unholy, the good from the bad, the wicked sinners from the redeemed saints. He gives man the ability to judge right from wrong so that we can make the right choices and understand truth. We can judge that the things of this world are not for us and when our brothers in Christ are not living according to God's Word and proceed accordingly.

These biblical terms are no longer used in biblical ways. If love is no longer a sacrificial desire to give oneself for the sake of another, we can easily make it a romanticized spectrum of whatever sin we wish to approve that week. If judgment is no longer about making prudent choices and holding ourselves and one another accountable, we can easily declare it simply a plank in your own eye.

> Judge not, that you be not judged. For with the judgment you pronounce you will be judged, and with the measure you use it will be measured to you. Why do you see the speck that is in your brother's eye, but do not notice the log that is in your own eye? Or how can you say to your brother, 'Let me take the speck out of your eye, 'when there is the log in your own eye? You hypocrite, first take the log out of your own eye, and then you will see clearly to take the speck out of your brother's eye." (Matthew 7:1–5).

These verses are often taken out of context as evidence against judgment. But the reality is that God has given us the ability to make judgment calls based on truth. The hypocritical judgment warned of in these verses is born out of self-righteousness and sinful

---

[40] "26. agapé," Bible Hub, accessed May 16, 2025, https://biblehub.com/greek/26.htm.

justification of our own actions.

Redefining these words has a significant impact on not only language but on society. Love is now just a flexible romantic notion, and judgment is a negative character trait, so there is no longer right and wrong. Well, the irony is that being judgmental is considered wrong despite the assertion that there is no right or wrong, but that's a discussion some folks aren't willing to have.

These two terms, especially applied together, become the one-two punch for a post- humanist. The idea there is no truth is a pile of manure, but instead of starting at the premise of biblical truth, Christians, lacking confidence in what they believe, fall for this and can't defend God's Word. They then accept the new definitions of these and other words because they don't have confidence in their ability to understand God's definition. Therefore, they think they must stay silent.

Another common technique that I used prior to my conversion and that many use today is the argument of creation versus evolution. Before I knew God, I went so far as to read the transcriptions of the cross-examination done by Clarence Darrow against William Jennings Bryant in the Scopes Monkey Trial to see how it played out. I wanted to know what questions Clarence Darrow used against others. Many people are so pitted against Christianity that they will do their research—religiously.

We have been trained to believe that evolution is the only way to describe our current form here. Beyond that, we don't understand or have the confidence to speak in favor of creationism. When a Christian lacks confidence in their awareness of the Bible, they can get tripped up. More likely, they will be ridiculed for not having a sixth-grade education, and even for successful adults, this jab can take us back to our insecure preteen selves. Ridicule not only breaks our confidence but has been employed against God's people all the way back to the Old Testament.

For example, Lot made some pretty poor decisions, but he was certainly ridiculed for the times he did stand in favor of truth. In Genesis 19, his sons-in-law did not take him seriously when he urged them to escape with them before the destruction of Sodom and Gomorrah. In addition, when the men came to seduce the angels, Lot refused, despite their anger.

In another example, in 1 Samuel 1, Eli the priest was so struck by Hannah's desperate prayer for a child that he criticized her and assumed she was drunk. Eli, a very flawed priest, was unaccustomed to seeing someone so passionate about their faith that they didn't care how they might appear to others.

The prophet Jeremiah was astonishingly and brutally ridiculed and mocked by the people of Israel when he warned them against the coming judgment. "Now Pashhur the priest, the son of Immer, who was chief officer in the house of the Lord, heard Jeremiah prophesying these things. Then Pashhur beat Jeremiah the prophet, and put him in the stocks that were in the upper Benjamin Gate of the house of the Lord" (Jeremiah 20:1–2).

Jeremiah suffered deeply for his willingness to stand for truth. Despite the pain and sacrifices, he truly loved the people of Judah enough that he was willing to experience all this pain. He was confident in the truth and in God's Word.

Ridicule doesn't even have to relate to our beliefs. Elisha was ridiculed for being bald.

And ridicule was a tool used in the New Testament against the apostles and even Jesus. A conflict between Peter and Paul enlightens us as to how those outside the gospel treat those within—as well as what it means when those who are following Christ concede to those arguments.

> But when Cephas came to Antioch, I opposed him to his face, because he stood condemned. For before certain men came from James, he was eating with the Gentiles; but when they came he drew back and separated himself, fearing the circumcision party. And the rest of the Jews acted hypocritically along with him, so that even Barnabas was led astray by their hypocrisy. But when I saw that their conduct was not in step with the truth of the gospel, I said to Cephas before them all, "If you, though a Jew, live like a Gentile and not like a Jew, how can you force the Gentiles to live like Jews?" (Galatians 2:11–14)

Peter worried that he might face rejection from the Jews if he didn't separate himself from those whom the Jews considered unclean. Rather than standing confidently for truth against their potential ridicule, he went ahead and caved, ignoring gospel truths for the sake of cultural comfort. He wasn't confident in his argument that circumcision was no longer required for followers of the one true God. As a result, he faced not mere ridicule but a solid rebuke. Paul's rebuke of Peter was perfectly legitimate, given the circumstances.

Indeed, we see a great many examples throughout Scripture and history. People have been ridiculed when they stood up for truth and for their faith. Likewise, they have been attacked when they didn't have the right answer, hurting their confidence.

But there is good news: You control this. While there is so much we cannot control, as long as God allows air in our lungs, we can make substantial strides in overcoming our lack of confidence. If you surrender to the work of the Holy Spirit in your life and if you commit to know your biblical reasons stronger than your political ones, you can gain confidence. If you humbly walk in the truth of God's Word, you have no reason to fear either failure or belligerence in how you respond.

You can take the following steps to do this:

1. First of all, be comfortable saying, "I don't know." This is the best answer when you genuinely aren't sure how to respond. So often, Christians will try to answer while not fully understanding the correct reasoning. When we say, "I don't know," it adds to our integrity, honesty, and genuineness. However, if we are going to maintain credibility, we should certainly add the phrase, "but I'll find out." Follow through on that. Find the answer. And when you do, you can get back with them and continue the discussion with the new information.

2. Secondly, a vital step in gaining confidence is to read your Bible. Read it systematically. Don't try to rush through a yearly Bible reading plan that just hurries you through whatever chapters happen to fit together. You don't need to put in a daily word count of the Bible. It's a continual, contextual, historical document. Take your time. If it takes you two years, then so be it.

3. Just read it. When you read it every day, God will honor your seeking by giving you understanding. The Holy Spirit will guide you and explain it to you. Don't focus on the type of translation. As long as it's an accurate translation,

read one you like, and the one you *will* read without getting overwhelmed.

4. Thirdly, start listening to podcasts and reading books on the topic of apologetics. Focus on the areas you struggle with the most. Start to understand those concepts that don't make much sense to you or that you don't necessarily like but believe to be true. It's okay to be uncomfortable with a theological concept even if you believe it's true. Sometimes we don't understand *why* God did something, so we wrestle with it. Trust that he will give you confidence about the subject, even if you still don't necessarily *like* that particular truth.[41]

5. Use more than one source and always verify it with God's Word. There's no point in diving into apologetics and then following whatever apologist you like without confirming if their views line up with Scripture. You can easily expect them to do the heavy lifting while you simply glean from their wisdom, but if you are going to have true confidence in the faith, you must do your part to understand.

6. As far as apologetics, we also need to train up our children in the faith and teach them how to defend the faith. We can open the doors for this by discussing apologetics with them and taking every opportunity to answer their questions. Understand the importance of a firm foundation and teach them Jesus before teaching morality (see appendix A).[42]

---

[41] I could offer other abundant examples, but let's take stealing, for example. We choose not to steal, and we obey God's Word about theft. We know what God's Word says (it's true), but we don't necessarily like that truth. Wouldn't it be nice if we could take what we want when we want it? Obviously, stealing is wrong biblically, politically, morally, and economically. But even if you have never stolen or been tempted to steal, everyone has items they'd like to own that they just can't afford. This same logic applies to many theological concepts and areas of sin. We may believe God's Word is true, but we just wish that particular issue weren't wrong. Christians who choose abstinence over same-sex attraction may believe the truth and choose obedience, but they may not necessarily *like* that truth. Someone struggling in their marriage may wish they could get a divorce, but they recognize that they simply don't have any valid reason to do so and that God has called them to commitment and sacrificial love whether or not they *like* that truth.

[42] One example of the value of teaching our children theology, Scripture, and a right understanding of Jesus as opposed to mere morality is the True Love Waits

7. Lastly, give up control. God will speak for us if we don't try to overshadow Him. He promises that in the Bible, but too often, we want to be the hero of the debate. We want to win.

8. Having a humble attitude will allow God to give you answers you didn't know he had given you, even as you read his Word. So focus on the truth and have confidence that God is greater than the arguments of others. He will give you the strength if you lean on him.

---

movement. In the evangelical church, youth were pushed to pursue abstinence as evidence of their faith. Many of these youth have now turned aside from the faith, often from bitterness that all the promises of a fulfilled sex life in marriage didn't come to pass. Their faith was founded on the theology of "by abstinence alone" rather than "by Christ alone." If we teach our children a right understanding of Christ and Scripture, moral values like abstinence outside of marriage are a natural byproduct.

For Reflection

1. When faced with a challenging or controversial topic, do you often hesitate to speak up? Why or why not? What can you do to build confidence in those moments?

2. Can you recall a time when you avoided discussing a biblical issue because you were afraid of being asked a difficult question? What was the outcome? How can you prepare yourself to handle challenging conversations with confidence?

3. How comfortable are you with acknowledging when you don't know the answer to a biblical or theological question? How do you handle such situations? How can you be more honest and confident in these moments?

4. In what ways do you actively engage with Scripture to build your confidence in discussing your faith?

5. How do you react when confronted with a counterargument or criticism about your beliefs? How can you respond with confidence, grounded in truth and love?

6. Have you ever felt that you needed to compromise when it comes to a biblical truth to avoid conflict or ridicule? What led you to that decision? How can you maintain boldness without compromising your convictions?

7. Identify resources (books, podcasts, etc.) that help you strengthen your ability to defend your faith. How can you use these tools more effectively?

8. When dealing with terms or concepts that are commonly redefined by others (e.g., love, judgment), how do you ensure you maintain a biblically accurate understanding? How can you stay grounded in Scripture during such discussions?

9. Can you describe a time when you felt confident in your biblical knowledge despite being ridiculed or challenged? What

helped you maintain that confidence?

10. Identify areas where you need more understanding of biblical and theological concepts. What specific steps are you taking to improve in those areas?

CHAPTER SEVEN

Lack of Consciousness

Sometimes, you just don't know. You might not be aware that something truly heinous or sinful is going on around you. You might not have heard about the awful behavior or wickedness that's taking place. In the pure effort to develop disciples and draw the congregation closer to God, your church might not be aware of something in the culture that's seriously problematic.

Another obstacle is preventing people from being bold—a lack of basic awareness. It is hard to be bold when you don't realize there is a problem. If someone was yelling at my child in front of me for something inane or incorrect, I would be bold and stand up to them. But if they were yelling at my child while I was ten miles away, I could not be bold in my response; I wouldn't even be aware it had happened until later, and that assumes my child tells me. Even then, we should investigate an incident to ensure that our awareness actually matches reality.

This lack of awareness often causes a massive disconnect. We may be passionate about a certain truth, but we don't even know about a chance to stand up for it. Our lack of awareness can be broken down into two parts:

- We may not be aware the problem is happening, or
- We may not be aware that we are seeing a problem

One evening, I was scrolling through Twitter, now X. A well-known national commentator had posted a video of a sex show under the guise of gay pride in Murfreesboro, Tennessee. I had not heard about it at all. I sent him an inbox message and told him he was wrong. This must be a Murfreesboro in another state.[43] He sent me the links to confirm that it was, indeed, my Murfreesboro, indicating it was I who was wrong.

At that point, I could not speak up or present solutions to the city managers and city council members. If I had known, I could have stood up for the protection of children before this even happened, before a public celebration of sex was underway in the streets of my city. But since I was unaware of it, I lacked boldness on the front end. I did ultimately speak with them to encourage them to use existing laws to prevent this from happening and protect our children. The city manager did his best, but the rest of the city government folded after a threat of a lawsuit from the ACLU.

Another time, I was speaking to a Wilson County group. Afterward, someone stood up and showed pictures of pornographic books in the middle school libraries. I had heard about this happening in larger cities and in more liberal states, but I was unaware this was happening right under my nose in the rural county where I have a business. I never would have imagined they could get away with such behavior in my backyard. It seemed as though others, like me, were also unaware. Because of our lack of awareness, we hadn't done anything to prevent it.

In Exodus 32, we see Moses up on Mount Sinai, enjoying the presence of the Lord, blissfully unaware the Israelites below were creating a golden calf for their worship. Later, God told Moses what they were doing so that Moses begged God to have mercy on them.

And yet, when Moses finally reached the base of the mountain, he utterly lost his temper and boldly destroyed the golden calf and made the people drink the remains.

> And the Lord said to Moses, "Go down, for your people, whom you brought up out of the land of Egypt, have corrupted themselves. They have turned aside quickly out of the way that I commanded them. They have made for themselves a golden calf and have worshiped it and sacrificed to it and said, 'These are your gods, O Israel, who

---

[43] There is a Murfreesboro in Tennessee, Arkansas, and North Carolina.

brought you up out of the land of Egypt!'" And the Lord said to Moses, "I have seen this people, and behold, it is a stiff-necked people . . . ."

And as soon as he came near the camp and saw the calf and the dancing, Moses's anger burned hot, and he threw the tablets out of his hands and broke them at the foot of the mountain. He took the calf that they had made and burned it with fire and ground it to powder and scattered it on the water and made the people of Israel drink it. (Exodus 32:7–9, 19–20)

This isn't the end of the story by any means, but it does show us how Moses initially responded when he suddenly became aware of a devastating sin he hadn't previously known about. It was a sin committed by his own people, even as he was receiving the Ten Commandments from God himself.

So how can we stop this from happening? How do we stand up against sin when we don't even know these things are taking place around us that we need to be bold against?

First of all, pay attention. Listen to the news—and not *just* mainstream media. Listen to them as well but also explore and investigate reporting and media coverage. Fact-check your sources beyond Snopes and Facebook fact-checking. It's not a conspiracy to say they have a definite progressive bias. That's just a fact of current media culture. It would be nice if the news reported facts instead of trying to create news.

You don't have to react to every situation. You need to explore how and when to react. Each circumstance requires careful consideration. God doesn't punish the same sins in the same way every time. He doesn't reward the same obedience in the same way every time. We, too, need to evaluate what is the right response for every situation.

For example, consider the following factors: Is this an isolated incident? Will this problem re-occur? Are there broader, more consequential implications beyond this moment? You don't need to stir up controversy and bring attention to the matter and possible support to the other side if it's an isolated matter. If, on the other hand, you do foresee the situation escalating into a long-term issue, you may need to evaluate your options.

Secondly, consider if this issue is a topic you are passionate about. In chapter 4, we looked at commitment. Are you committed to this? Are you going to continue standing up for this, or will you back down when it gets hard, when it's inconvenient, or in the frame of the previous chapter, if you lose confidence? You don't want to make a stink over an issue if you don't plan to follow through. Consider this before you dive in. After all, if you aren't going to finish this battle you're starting, it's probably not your fight.

Thirdly, and most importantly, ask God if he wants you to be involved. Most of the time, if the thought of involvement is coming to your mind and you can't shake it, this means he wants you to be involved. Listen and wait for that clarity instead of just diving in because of momentary rage. Be sure his still, small voice is urging you to move forward.

Next, ask how you should be involved. What do you believe God wants you to do? Are those actions consistent with what you find in Scripture? (And remember, we're probably looking at actions more consistent with the New Testament disciples preaching despite risk and less the idea of radical Old Testament examples, such as circumcising and subsequently executing an entire male population in revenge or sending flaming foxes to burn down their crops. See Genesis 34 for the brutal response of Jacob's sons to their sister's assault. See Judges 15 for Samson's response when his wife was given to another man.)

Don't let your cause become an idol.[44] This is easy to do when we see an injustice or something clearly against God. So often, we find ourselves taking up a fight in his name, only to then let it consume us. So pay close attention. God may be asking you to stand firm in this, but if it overwhelms you to the point of idolatry, you may need to limit yourself. This takes wisdom and strength to know if you're crossing the line from passion and justice into obsession.

Lastly, remember to use your circle of influence. That's more than enough. You don't need a national platform. Plenty of people out there with big platforms are making a difference, and maybe you've been called to be one, but most of us are meant to have a smaller circle of influence closer to home.

Don't be afraid to start small. If God wants to use you in a bigger context, the opportunities will come. Remember that our

---

[44] I address this more in depth in chapter 9 of my book *On the Duty of Christian Civil Disobedience*.

behavior in the small circumstances, the little things, is important in determining how we behave in the bigger ones.

Another situation to consider also ties in with a lack of confidence. We are not always conscious of a serious problem because of our ignorance of God's Word. We may not even realize we have a problem. Our lack of knowledge or how easily we can be conned by non-Christians has convinced us there is not a problem to begin with. Then, we cannot be bold against those issues. When wickedness presents itself, we are unaware that we need to say anything. The awareness of God's Word and of the moral degeneracy in our community and culture go hand in hand.

Many times, this lack of knowledge is because we have been so thoroughly tricked to believe that good is bad and bad is good. This is clearly a problem as the Bible calls out these people who work to confuse others and convince them to fall for a lie. "Woe to those who call evil good and good evil, who put darkness for light and light for darkness, who put bitter for sweet and sweet for bitter!" (Isaiah 5:20). God was not telling us this theoretically. Knowing the Bible is a practical tool for us to use, God warns us not to become these people. Unfortunately, as with anything wicked, these people do exist.

We saw this in Germany in the 1930s. Ninety-five percent of Nazis were baptized Christians,[45] as I discussed further in my book *On the Duty of Christian Civil Disobedience*.[46] Many of those that committed the atrocities of the Holocaust, or at least helped support it, did so not realizing they were committing evil. The culture had manipulated them into believing it was the right thing, even the Christian thing, to do. Evil was called good, and the average person fell for it. They didn't see how unholy and vile it truly was.

How often do we see that in our modern times and culture? How many people grew up in church and still call themselves Christians but support ideologies contrary to their faith? They don't want to rock the boat with controversial opinions that may get them declared unloving. They don't want to appear too political—or on the wrong side of politics from their friends. They don't want to stand against culture, especially when they can derive pleasure from it. Half of Christians in the United States say that casual sex is

---

[45] D. L. Bergen, "Twisted Cross," 2000, The University of North Carolina Press.
[46] Peter Demos, *On the Duty of Christian Civil Disobedience* (Five Stone Press, 2022).

acceptable.[47] Tim Tebow was attacked, mocked, and shamed for not engaging in this behavior.[48]

We often look back at the Holocaust and wonder how it happened. After all, knowing just how horrific it was, it's honestly hard to believe the majority of an entire nation would go along with that type of genocide. We see genocides taking place in many parts of the world throughout history, from Cambodia to China to Rwanda to countless other nations and examples. But oftentimes, these are based on tribes and power.

During the Holocaust, one man convinced a whole people group that a small minority was such a great threat that they must be exterminated. His own hatred, despite having Jewish blood himself, influenced and manipulated an entire government system. A new structure for education was adopted. A method of media propaganda was created. And over six million people were murdered because of their race, their disabilities, or other traits deemed undesirable.

How could this possibly have happened? In this country, we see it all the time—albeit on a much smaller scale thus far. People have always been demonized for their beliefs, but it's hard to ignore how significant the divide has become since Trump became President in 2016. We are divided by race, politics, ally-ship of whatever sort, even our views on the efficacy of face masks. Regular people who believe everyone is equal were told by the media to cut off friends based on these insignificant disagreements.

But people don't want to rock the boat. They don't want to go against popular opinion. They cozy up to leaders, many of whom claim to be Christians, who hold views that are heinously unbiblical. Then, when the leaders allow and even promote sin, according to the Bible, the average person who follows them thinks it must be okay. After all, this person is leading the way in their faith, aren't they? They're doing God's work, aren't they? Who are we to question them when they seem to know so much more than we do about the Bible? And not only from a religious, churchy approach but a scholarly one!

---

[47] Jeff Diamant, "Half of U.S. Christians say casual sex between consenting adults is sometimes or always acceptable," Pew Research, August 31, 2020, https://www.pewresearch.org/short-reads/2020/08/31/half-of-u-s-christians-say-casual-sex-between-consenting-adults-is-sometimes-or-always-acceptable/.
[48] Jemele Hill, "Tebow practices what he preaches," ESPN, July 27, 2009, https://www.espn.com/espn/page2/story?sportCat=ncf&page=hill/090724.

Some progressive leaders claim to be pastors and ministers while living a homosexual lifestyle. They justify that the Bible doesn't actually condemn their choice of a partner. With claims that the Bible has been poorly translated into English—and apparently every single other language—they insist we've misread it all these years. Some say that verses condemning homosexuality were inserted later. Still others declare that homosexuality itself wasn't being condemned but that the Bible is actually referring to attempts at assault in most instances. One such example is when Lot defends the angels against the men of Sodom who wanted to use them physically (Genesis 19:4–10).

When words and language can be redefined, anything can be twisted. Consider how many politicians claim Catholicism as their religion only to promote abortion until birth. Is it truly possible to be a believer in Christ, beholden to the Scriptures, reading Psalm 139 among others, and claiming it's all right for a child to be ripped apart in the womb with their body parts sold to science? To be fair, plenty of self-proclaimed Protestants fall into this category as well.

We're told how cruel it is to force a woman to have a child if she doesn't want to with examples of all the women traumatized by assault. The argument insists that it's not fair to make them give birth to a child who may look like her attacker.

One trend is to use sexual assault to justify a number of topics because it is so horrific to our minds that it easily twists our emotions. Likewise, it's used to humanize pedophiles to differentiate those who would attack a child from those who merely have an attraction but would never commit such a heinous crime. Those who would engage in assault are vicious; those who merely have the attraction are just another color on the flag.[49]

It's disturbing how easily people can fall into these traps—and many more similar traps of other twisted topics. And when a person claims to be a Christian authority has fooled their followers and drawn in those who want to hear that they are justified without being sanctified, it's quite simple to demonize those who believe sanctification is a part of the process as well. People don't want to let go of their sin. First, they must acknowledge their sin. They have to accept it's real. No one wants to admit that.

---

[49] Alia E. Dastagir, "The complicated research behind pedophilia," January 10, 2022, *USA Today*, https://www.usatoday.com/story/life/health-wellness/2022/01/10/pedophiles-pedophilia-sexual-disorder/8768423002/.

The voices of truth and reason will inevitably face the same criticism Jeremiah faced when he stood up for truth. Even as he proclaimed the Word of God as a prophet, he was relentlessly mocked and disregarded by the wicked people.

> "For from the least to the greatest of them, everyone is greedy for unjust gain; and from prophet to priest, everyone deals falsely.
>
> They have healed the wound of my people lightly, saying, 'Peace, peace,' when there is no peace.
>
> Were they ashamed when they committed abomination?
>
> No, they were not at all ashamed; they did not know how to blush.
>
> Therefore they shall fall among those who fall; at the time that I punish them, they shall be overthrown," says the Lord. (Jeremiah 6:13–15).

But there is a solution to at least prevent ourselves from falling into the trap of falsely declaring peace where there is none. The best way to overcome this is to read your Bible systematically. It may sound repetitive when this is, so often, the solution offered. But it's a crucial aspect of living righteously when the rest of the world ignores the truth.

You will not get all the answers overnight. At times, I have read the Bible when I woke up to a problem that I didn't know about when I first became a Christian. It's all right not to understand everything right away, but it's important to make the effort and work toward understanding it.

This is similar to when you were a child. You didn't know everything your parents were saying as you didn't understand all the words. Soon, you recognize basic words that fit your needs, and then you learn more, and your vocabulary increases. Before long, your vocabulary will grow to a higher level, based on the effort you put into it.

For me, the order of understanding was:

1. I read it in the Bible but did not recognize it as contrary to the world.
2. The problem—or sin—occurred around me, but I said

nothing or didn't notice.

3. I read the Bible again and found the problem.

This was just preparing me for the next time I came across the issue. Then, if I did see it, I could make an informed decision as to whether God wanted me to take a stand. This, of course, happened based on the method we already looked at for distinguishing how to respond in light of a problem.

In reality, we may not have a conscious awareness of the problems around us, but it doesn't have to be that way. We don't need to live in deception. We don't have to tell ourselves that either the problem isn't happening or that the problem isn't a problem. If we are aware of what's going on around us by simply staying informed and if we have a heartfelt understanding of Scripture through diligent study, we can make the right choice at the right time and stand boldly for our faith.

For Reflection

1. Do you regularly engage with local news and community boards and activities? Are you actively seeking to understand local events and policies that may require a faith-based response? Actively participate in town hall meetings or local forums to stay informed about what's happening in your area.

2. Do you set up alerts or follow diverse news sources to stay updated on various topics? Are you actively seeking diverse sources to stay informed and avoid bias? Make it a habit to check multiple perspectives to get a fuller picture of current events.

3. Think about your engagement with educational resources. How can you expand your knowledge to better understand and engage with current social and cultural issues?_

4. Do you dedicate time to regular, systematic Bible study to deepen your understanding of Scripture? How can you apply this to current societal issues?

5. Do you engage in open discussions with others in your community or faith group about current events and issues? How can you contribute to thoughtful and respectful conversations about cultural and social issues?

6. Do you volunteer for or support organizations that align with your values and work toward addressing social issues? Consider your involvement in causes that align with your faith. How can you become more active in helping address social issues that are important to you?

7. Do you hold local leaders accountable by understanding their policies and positions? Engage in civic activities and communicate with elected officials to express concerns or support for specific issues.

8. If you are doing a good job staying involved, then check your motivations and actions to ensure they align with your values and the

teachings of your faith. Are your actions rooted in biblical principles, or are they influenced by personal passions?

CHAPTER EIGHT

Cynicism

The next obstacle has to do with our attitude. And while we often don't think of our attitudes as being a problem or we justify our reasoning for feeling a specific way about a topic, it's important to remember that our self-justification doesn't excuse our poor responses.

Charles Swindoll has some valuable thoughts on the matter in his poem "Attitude."

> The longer I live, the more I realize the impact of attitude on life.
>
> Attitude, to me, is more important than facts.
>
> It is more important than the past, than education, than money, than circumstances, than failures, than successes, than what other people think or say or do. It is more Important than appearance, giftedness or skill.
>
> It will make or break a company: a church . . . a home. The remarkable thing is, we have a choice every day, regarding the attitude we will embrace for that day.
>
> We cannot change the inevitable.
>
> The only thing we can do is play on the one string we have, and that is our attitude.
>
> I am convinced that life is 10% what happens to me and 90% how I react to it.

And so it is with you . . . we are in charge of our attitudes.[50]

Consider these words and what they mean in your day-to-day life. Are you letting your attitude get in the way of living a Christlike life? Is it possible you don't even notice some areas where you've found yourself growing complacent? Or even cynical? Many Christians claim to believe in the Bible. They claim to believe in prayer and God's miracles as well—until it comes time to read their Bibles, faithfully pray, or ask God for a miracle. Then, suddenly, it seems fairly useless to have faith in any of those things. Our attitude toward the truth of Scripture, the power of prayer, and the ability of God to perform miracles in our lives is met with the idea that it won't really do any good to ask.

The harsh realities of this world have left us cynical, assuming that since we don't have the power to stop our own hardships, God must not have that power either. Those of us who claim to be Christians would never say that aloud. We would never acknowledge our inner doubt or admit that "God can't do it," but our attitudes speak much more loudly than our words when it comes to our theological values.

If we are in need of a miracle and are too cynical to pray, we are making a statement about his goodness that doesn't reflect well on us. We think that if God wanted us to have that miracle, he'd just do it anyway, even if we didn't pray. Certainly, God is sovereign and can do whatever He wants, but if He leads us to pray and seek Him, it's because He wants us to pray and lean in. It's not for his sake but for ours.

We say we value the Bible, but we memorized John 3:16 as a child and assume we already know what's important. We're evidencing the value we actually place on God's Word. We are not prioritizing Scripture in our daily lives. Cynicism creeps into our spiritual walk in our day-to-day interactions. And, unfortunately, a cynical nature can only prove that we don't value what we ought.

Consider how easy it is to dismiss responsibility when outcomes feel inevitable or unchangeable. After the tragic attack on

---

[50] Dallas Theological Seminary, "Attitude – Charles R. Swindoll," sermon, May 31, 2012, YouTube, https://www.youtube.com/watch?v=9lnvN0buts4. Note that the poem originated years earlier but is quoted here by the author.

the US Embassy in Benghazi that left four Americans dead, then–Secretary of State Hillary Clinton responded to questioning by asking, "What difference does it make?"[51] Her statement became infamous not because people doubted the tragedy itself but because it appeared to dismiss the value of understanding *why* it happened. That attitude—whether in politics or in our own hearts—mirrors the spiritual apathy we sometimes carry. We say we trust God and care about His truth, but when it comes time to act, we shrug. "What difference would it make?" That same cynicism keeps us from boldness in prayer, obedience, or witness. But boldness in Christ demands we push past resignation and believe that *truth and responsibility do matter*—even when the outcome seems beyond our control.

We feel this way about so many circumstances but tell ourselves otherwise. We say we care; we say that our cause matters to us. We say that we trust God in all things, but we don't even know how to step out and be bold. We fear what might happen if we do try to stand up or pray for a miracle and it doesn't happen, so it's easier to say, "Sure, of course God can do miracles—but I'm not going to pray for one. What difference does my prayer make?"

We may be cynical for a number of reasons from doubt to insecurity to fear to anger. So many events and beliefs can lead us down this path. But do we believe God is true or not?

On my show *Uncommon Sense in Current Times*,[52] I interview many bold people. I often ask them, "So what?" It's a valuable question. I don't ask them because I'm cynical about their opinions; I ask because we all need to be able to answer this. What is the reason? What difference does it really make? Why should you do this if we are all doomed anyway? Why does it matter that we stand up for what's right if Revelation already tells us how it's going to end? Why be bold when we live in a broken world that's overrun by evil anyway?

So what?

Even if they believe no good is to be found in our current

---

[51] ABC News, "Hillary Clinton's Fiery Moment at Benghazi Hearing," YouTube video, 2:22, January 23, 2013, https://www.youtube.com/watch?v=TC0AKNQBV80.

[52] Peter Demos, *Uncommon Sense in Current Times*, accessed May 16, 2025, https://www.peterdemos.org/uncommon-sense-in-current-times.

culture, many of my guests are hopeful that a few people can be convinced. And if a few people can be convinced of the truth, this helps spread the word. The boldness of the few can lead to the awakening of the many.

We aren't taking a step of boldness because we believe our single argument if aired on all the mainstream media networks, YouTube, X, and Rumble, will suddenly change the minds of every person in Western society. We don't do it because we believe we are so convincing or have the one angle that no one else is talking about, the one angle that will convince everyone around us. We step out in boldness because we want to plant a seed that the Holy Spirit will water. We are bold because that is what we are called to do. We can easily answer the "What difference does it make?" question when we know the difference is our obedience or disobedience. We can easily answer when we know a lack of boldness will lead to no change at all, whereas a choice for boldness may lead to change.

A seed planted in the wrong conditions has a greater chance of sprouting and growing than a seed not planted at all. The first may lead to an apple tree that one day bears a significant amount of fruit or it could end up withering. The apple seed unplanted will never be anything but squandered potential. We don't decide if the planted seed grows; that's up to God. But the unplanted seed doesn't even have the chance.

Imagine the potential for cynicism among the small group of leaders within the first church in Rome. They were a tiny group of believers in Christ, facing the most powerful empire in the world. Yet they pushed forward a few people at a time. They made claims about a man who disrupted society and then came back from a horrific death. They didn't need one thousand followers on Instagram, Facebook, or Fox News to tell the nation.

They just needed to be bold, to show their passion for Christ, and to honor what God had called them to do. Little by little, one person at a time, then in large groups, the Holy Spirit worked through their boldness. Jesus is the most famous person in history. Other religions even try to use his name for their own purposes because they know his name alone has power.

But being bold is not about quantity but about quality. It's not about results but the process. As humans used to immediate results, we expect to see the answer right away, and sometimes we just don't get the answer we want. Then, the next time we need to pray about a problem or go to our Bible for comfort and confidence, we don't totally trust it. We would verbally say that we know the value of God's Word and prayer, but in our hearts, it's a last resort.

Art Thomas with Supernatural Truth Productions leads a healing ministry and teaches on the subject.[53] He has said he has ministered healing in Jesus's name to an entire room of about twenty people, except for one person, when he prayed. He doesn't know why that one person wasn't healed, but they were not. Yet he still prays for healing. He knows God is in control, that God makes the final decisions. Instead of growing cynical about the one perceived failure, he has faith that God hears his prayers and wants us to be healed.

When we think taking action does no good, it then becomes a self-fulfilling prophecy because we choose not to act, so nothing happens. Then we think we were right—after all, nothing happened anyhow. In this way, we justify our inaction and convince ourselves it was the wise choice. We believe we saved our efforts for when they are really needed. That's when we will be bold.

I look at my own life and testimony. People were praying for me for many years, hoping I would one day be redeemed and saved by Jesus. Some people were praying for me for over twenty years. And yet, I was in my forties before I actually got saved. Meanwhile, others said they didn't pray for me because they thought it would do no good. They thought it was hopeless that I would ever surrender to God. Imagine if the first group did not pray. Would I not have been saved until my fifties, or would I ever have been saved at all? Without their prayers, would I ever have been drawn to Christ?

However, imagine if the cynical Christians who saw no hope in me had joined with those who were diligently praying. Would I have been saved in my mid-thirties? No one knows. But their cynicism did not help. While I don't question the way God did bring me into salvation, I do know that those who were too cynical to believe I would ever know God did nothing to benefit the situation.

Sometimes we think a situation didn't work simply because it hasn't yet worked in our favor. And it's possible that it *never will* work in our favor, but it is still working in God's plan.

---

[53] https://www.supernaturaltruth.com/art-thomas.

Hard Lessons

After receiving extensive counsel from godly businessmen, I once hired someone who was supposed to help me grow my restaurant business. I prayed for the right person and eventually did a nationwide search. It was a humbling place to be in but seemed like a wise business decision, finding someone to run operations and handle some of the day-to-day tasks so I could focus on my role. In every way, it seemed like the right thing to do.

I prayed over the six candidates, and one was the clear choice. My wife and I prayed before the meeting with him and his wife, and it just seemed obvious. The meeting went well; he and his wife seemed like great people. And we did everything the way that a wise, Christian business owner should do them—through prayer, diligently seeking God's guidance, and waiting for the Holy Spirit to give us the go ahead.

Following this, I went through a time of medical issues, and I relied on this man to do what he'd been hired to do for the company. In the midst of what I was dealing with, I felt like I was walking through a medication fog. Something didn't quite seem right with the company, but I couldn't pinpoint it. Everyone liked the guy, and nothing stood out as a red flag. And why would there be a problem? God had made it clear I was meant to hire him. Surely he was the right choice for running the operations of my business.

Eventually, God miraculously healed me, and as I came out of that fog, I started to see that this man and his decisions really weren't as they appeared on the surface.

Within a couple of years, this man almost bankrupted us. I knew I had followed God's guidance, I had pursued wisdom, and I had done everything right in my approach. And he nearly ruined us. I had to terminate him, and it took another four years to start coming out of the mess.

And then, just as we were recovering from the financial chaos he had led us into, COVID happened. We could have gone into COVID financially strong and easily rebounded from that setback, but we were only just getting back on our feet after his decisions. COVID, then, only compounded our business problems, and truthfully, I am still dealing with the problems he created.

But I wasn't just upset with him about his decisions. I was angry with God. I felt betrayed. One early morning, unable to sleep, I went for a walk. I let God know exactly how I felt and what was on my mind. I made it clear I was unhappy with his job performance, how he had led me through all this even though I had tried to be wise and hand over my decisions to him.

"I did everything right, and I got problems in return," I kept telling him. There's no need to elaborate on some of the other things I may have said. I thought, *What difference does it make to even pray when I get nothing but problems in return?* After all, when you do everything right, you expect God to reward you and give you grace in the midst of storms. You expect God to honor your choice to let him have his way. And I'd let him have His way. I'd gone with the candidate he clearly showed me, and now I was suffering for it.

A few weeks later, I was leaving a breakfast meeting and walking to my car. Out of nowhere, God said, "I did not bring him there for you. I brought him there for him."

I felt terrible—like I was punched in the gut. I immediately repented of my anger and how I'd been treating God so cynically. I'd been spending all that time feeling sorry for myself and being angry that God had led me down that path, as if he'd made a mistake. In reality, none of it was about me. God had allowed me to go through all that because he was trying to do a work in the man I'd hired.

We look to ourselves in the midst of struggle, and often, others assume our problems are the consequence of our own failures. But sometimes God has a greater purpose for not answering our prayers or for answering them in a way that doesn't benefit us.

Did Job ever find out why God allowed him to suffer so greatly? Reading through the book of Job, we can see that, really, it had nothing to do with Job. He did everything he could to honor God. But he suffered because, through his suffering, God was glorified and made a stark point to the enemy about his will. Job had nothing to do with it, even when everyone else assumed his own sin was the problems. Even when his wife wanted him to curse God and die. Even when he felt hopeless. Even when his friends accused him.

Plenty of cynicism surrounded Job, but we mainly see his grief. He couldn't understand. He questioned why God would allow these disasters, but he never cynically sighed and said, "Fine, if you're just going to treat me this way, I might as well sin!"

Job 38–40 is a stunning work of theology and poetry. (See especially Job 38:4–11.) When challenged, God lists his glory but ultimately begs the question of Job 40:2: "Shall a faultfinder contend with the Almighty? He who argues with God, let him answer it."

As I felt sorry for my circumstances and shared my anger with God, I let myself become cynical, thinking all my prayers had done no good anyway. But God, in his mercy, answered me. And like Job, it led to my repentance. (See Job 42:1–6.)

I realized my cynicism does no good. But my boldness in praying for others and letting them see my trust in God does much good. We cannot be cynical just because things don't work in our favor. Even if it feels foolish or counterintuitive, we have to be bold and trust in God.

For Reflection

1. Reflecting on the insights from Charles Swindoll and the chapter's discussion on cynicism, consider a situation in your life when you've faced disappointment or unmet expectations, particularly in relation to your faith. Describe a specific instance when you felt disillusioned or cynical about a spiritual practice or belief (e.g., prayer, Bible study, or trusting in God's plan). What was the situation, and how did your attitude affect your response or actions?

2. How might a shift in attitude, as described by Swindoll, impact your approach to similar situations in the future? Consider both practical changes you might make and deeper, internal shifts in perspective.

3. When faced with challenges or setbacks, how do you typically respond? Do you find yourself questioning the effectiveness of prayer or the value of Scripture?

4. Can you identify instances when your attitude of cynicism has led to a lack of action or faith? How did this affect the outcome of those situations?

5. When you pray for a significant outcome, do you genuinely believe in the possibility of a miracle, or do you approach prayer with a sense of skepticism or doubt?

6. Do you actively engage with the Bible, seeking new insights and understanding, or do you assume you already know everything important? How does your approach reflect your attitude toward its relevance?

7. Are there areas in your life where you feel hesitant to act boldly because you doubt the effectiveness of your actions? How does this impact your boldness and actions in your faith journey?

8. When you feel that God has directed you to take a specific action, but it does not produce the desired result, how do you

respond? Do you become disheartened or question God's guidance? Think about moments when God's guidance led to unexpected outcomes. How can you learn to trust Him more fully?

9. Have you noticed that your cynical attitude impacts those around you, possibly discouraging them from taking action or pursuing their faith? How can you change your perspective to positively impact those around you?

10. How do you handle moments when you recognize your own cynicism? What steps can you take to shift your attitude and embrace a more faithful, hopeful approach?

CHAPTER NINE

Comparison

The next obstacle we have to overcome is an increasingly difficult one: the issue of comparison. When we compare ourselves to our past or to others, we find that we lose joy. We lose the reality of who we are now and where God has us at this moment.

But we also start to lose the ability to be bold. We think, *I cannot be as bold as that person, so why bother being bold at all?* And once we go down that path of questioning ourselves and our ability to be bold, we just want to give up.

Maybe we have been passionate about an issue in the past and stood up for it, but our circumstances have changed, and we don't feel we can do that again. Maybe you're too burned out from a lifetime of fighting for justice, so you give up because you are worn out and exhausted. You feel like a different person.

We change over time, and we become discouraged when an opportunity arises when we feel we need to go out of our way to take a bold step—but we just don't have it in us. Maybe our priorities have changed, perhaps due to having kids or maybe because of a health crisis.

If we see someone we admire who is going out of their way to do big things, we are intimidated and stop trying. It could even be a friend or a relative. We feel like we are in their shadow now. If we suddenly try to stand up for something, we'll just look like we're trying to be like them and will look foolish if we don't accomplish something special. People will assume we're riding the other person's coattails in an attempt to compete with their giftings.

Social media does not help the situation either. We look at pictures of our friends and frenemies, and we see their smiling, happy family. Resentment overwhelms us. We look at what they have and start chasing what we envy instead of what God wants for us. Sooner or later, God's vision for our lives becomes a blur, and we no longer have a reason to be bold anymore.

Abundant insecurities could stand in the way. But whether you are comparing your current situation to yourself in a different stage of life or comparing yourself to other people, it's not healthy or productive. Being sad that you don't weigh the same as you did at graduation isn't going to help you lose weight now, and looking at someone's exciting vacation photos on Facebook doesn't gain you a passport stamp. Comparison is unproductive and only hinders our ability to live today to the fullest.

In fact, comparison led to the very first murder recorded in history when Cain killed Abel. Abel's sacrifice found favor with God while Cain's did not (Genesis 4:1–16). Comparison led to a deceiver receiving a blessing that his father meant for someone else (Jacob and Esau in Genesis 25:19–34; 27:1–15). It led to that deceiver showing unbelievable favoritism toward one of his wives and her eldest son (Rachel and Leah and eventually Joseph versus his brothers Genesis 29:15–35; 30:1–24).

While God used each of these situations and turned them around for his good, a whole lot of sin came out of the wickedness of comparison. The people who engaged in their trivial competitive desires were harmed, and so were others. Just because God can turn any situation for his glory and our good doesn't mean that their sin was excused without repentance.

Personally, I struggle with comparison when it comes to working out and exercising. I want to work out so I can be stronger as I get older. That way, my kids hopefully won't have to take care of me, or I can at least delay that possibility. If I make the effort to take care of my body, I could be sparing them that burden. I also want to make certain I am prepared if I have to live under persecution. At least, not by any fault of my own. And it doesn't hurt that I'd like the way I would look over time.

I am truly motivated to pursue this kind of fitness. I know my reasons. I know that it's valuable. I know we are blessed to have the bodies God has given us, and it's important to take care of them and use them rightly. So my goals are just. My reasons are valid. And my plan is secure.

But then, I look at these muscle-bound guys at the gym or on the cover of fitness magazines at the grocery store, and I realize that no matter what I do—outside of steroids or human growth hormones—I will never look like that. My genetics will not allow me to even enter a muscle-building contest. I find myself discouraged by this reality, and I wonder why I can't be like them. I wonder if all my efforts are pointless since I'll never be that strong or ripped, no matter how hard I try. So I stop going to the gym and give up.

Who does this hurt? Well, not those guys at the gym who are busy taking care of themselves. They could care less whether or not I show up. It only hurts me and possibly my kids later when I'm not able to be as independent as I'd like to be in later years. With this in mind, it hurts the goal I was busy pursuing. All the reasons I had for working toward this have been completely overwhelmed by my comparison and subsequent insecurity. What I thought I wanted clearly didn't mean as much to me as I had said. I now don't think it's worth it to be the best I can be—if it means I can't achieve that unattainable goal of being like the pros.

Comparison is obviously not a positive option when it comes to standing boldly. When we compare ourselves to others who are being bold for Christ, the same is true. I cannot be like that other person I admire, so why be bold at all?

Who does this mentality hurt? Again, not the person I am comparing myself with but me. And it hurts the goal of winning people to Christ.

The Bible is clear. We don't compare ourselves to others. We just step out and be bold. Among the countless verses throughout the Old and New Testaments, the following remind us of the value of obeying the command to boldness.

- "And when they had prayed, the place in which they were gathered together was shaken, and they were all filled with the Holy Spirit and continued to speak the word of God with boldness" (Acts 4:31).
- "Paul entered the synagogue and spoke boldly there for three months, arguing persuasively about the kingdom of

God" (Acts 19:8).

- "Accordingly, though I am bold enough in Christ to command you to do what is required, yet for love's sake I prefer to appeal to you—I, Paul, an old man and now a prisoner also for Christ Jesus" (Philemon 1:8–9).

- "David also said to Solomon his son, 'Be strong and courageous, and do the work. Do not be afraid or discouraged, for the Lord God, my God, is with you. He will not fail you or forsake you until all the work for the service of the temple of the Lord is finished'" (1 Chronicles 28:20).

While dozens of other verses could be included, the most consistent trend among them all is the fact that we are commanded to boldness—not that we are commanded to be bolder than someone else or to do better than someone else. That's not what God has called us to. He has simply called us to preach the gospel and to live in obedience according to his Word.

Scripture never tells us that Paul and Peter are arguing over which of them has preached to more people. They argue over theological concepts and approaches or methods of reaching the lost, but they are never recorded as debating over who has brought more souls to Christ. That idea is along the lines of Legolas and Gimli in the movie *The Lord of the Rings* when the two keep track of how many enemies they have each slain. Despite their friendship, they always want to outdo one another. This is contrary to what we see depicted in the boldness of those in Scripture who follow Jesus.

Being bold can serve a great purpose that we can't always see. Sometimes our boldness is about planting seeds. We don't always see where this impacts other people around us, but it does often impact them nevertheless. It could be twenty years later and a friend has moved to the other side of the world and you've lost contact before they finally turn to Christ, even though you were the first person to ever share his Word with them.

Does it matter? Do you need the gratification of knowing you contributed to their salvation? Of course not. Because salvation is achieved by the mercy of Christ alone, so your contribution of planting the seeds was only a matter of obedience. If you treasure that obedience, you are treasuring what matters. "Do not lay up for yourselves treasures on earth, where moth and rust destroy and where thieves break in and steal, but lay up for yourselves treasures in Heaven, where neither moth nor rust destroys and where thieves do not break in and steal. For where your treasure is, there your heart will be also" (Matthew 6:19–24).

In my youth, two individuals showed boldness with me: a girl I dated a couple of times and a server who worked for me. (I even interviewed him later on my show, *Uncommon Sense in Current Times*.)[54] Both individuals stood up for Christ and did not attack me, even when I deserved it or made fun of them for their beliefs. I was so impressed, even though they did not convince me to follow Jesus. I noticed how they handled it, certainly boldly and absolutely without belligerence. So despite the fact that I didn't immediately turn to Christ, those two people still impacted me.

When I made the decision to surrender my life to Jesus, I recognized their influence, and I could emulate their behavior. I was also extremely fortunate in that I could call both of them and ask for their forgiveness. Not everyone has that opportunity, but if you do, it's a wonderful blessing to thank those who made that kind of a difference and to apologize for anything you may have said or done to hurt them.

Once we have turned to Jesus, we now get to learn from those who planted the seeds in our hearts. We don't need to be foolish and compare ourselves with them but rather can emulate them.

If I had made the decision to follow Christ and thought about those two, I had multiple choices. I could have done exactly what I did. Or I could have gone out and had as many pushy conversations with unbelievers as possible. Why would I do the latter? Because if it took those two people to plant seeds in my heart, now I needed to go out and plant seeds in at least two other people's hearts to prove that I, too, am a good Christian. I couldn't let their faith outshine mine. Surely, I now needed to prove I was just as capable of sharing the gospel as they were. Or perhaps, that would just be the belligerent response to the entire situation.

I look at evangelism like a big bucket. Everyone in life has a big

---

[54] Peter Demos, "Giving your life to the Lord and being a new Christian in an evil world: Interview with Jeremy Myers," *Uncommon Sense in Current Times*, accessed July 7, 2025, https://rumble.com/v4evv15-giving-your-life-to-the-lord-and-being-a-new-christian-in-an-evil-world.html.

bucket that starts out empty. When someone finally sees the truth and has a relationship with Jesus, their bucket is filled with water and overflows. Each person's bucket is a different size. Sometimes parents help fill the bucket. Other people may not have the blessing of parents with water, so it could take a little longer before the bucket even collects a few drops.

Some people add water to their bucket by the gallons, and others add water to it in cups or even milliliters and drops. If the person dies before the bucket overflows, they never get to know Jesus and the water remained stagnant and unusable. But if I add a small amount to someone's bucket, it may be added to the large amount that someone else contributed. My small amount could be the amount of water that causes the bucket to overflow.

Someone in your life might not be receptive to the gospel. Your mutual friend has continually been bold with humility and grace, and this person just keeps rejecting it. Because they keep rejecting it, you figure it's not really worth the effort to talk to them about the Lord. (This relates to the previous chapter on cynicism.) But maybe this person is three drops away from being full. Maybe they need three drops from a different source instead of your mutual friend who has repeatedly shard the gospel with them.

Being bold adds water to the buckets around you. But don't compare how much water you add to what other people are adding, or you may miss out on the opportunity to help someone's bucket overflow.

A Tale of Two Missions

Let me give you an example of two mission trips.

The missionary and his team arrived in the city, and no one was there to greet them. They could not meet with any of the religious leaders there as there didn't seem to be any, so they went to a local gathering place, and they met one woman. Later, the missionary cast out a demon, and he was beaten and jailed, but while in jail, he shared the gospel with the jailor, who was receptive, and the missionary was then freed and could leave the city.

In the second scenario, a different story plays out.

The missionary arrived and went to the religious leaders who subsequently rejected him. Yet he continued to preach the gospel and grew a thriving church. Ultimately, he converted another religious leader and his family. He was there eighteen months, teaching and growing the church. On the surface, if I were to compare these two mission trips, the second one seems much more successful than the first one. I would give up and never try again if I had been the missionary leader of the first trip. My boldness resulted in two conversions, a cool miracle, and being beaten and jailed. While there are a couple of victories in there, it wasn't the most glamorous result.

Can you imagine coming back and telling your friends and your church this story? They would not want you to present this story to the church or share about the trip or about how the outreach went, especially if they had helped fundraise for the journey. Instead, you would be met with skepticism and maybe even some irritation.

"I witnessed and two people got saved!"

"Only two?"

"Yes—but it was amazing."

"You spent time and money for two people?"

You get the point. It is not worth the comparison to even post on Facebook.

With the other mission trip, I managed to get a bigger church and a visit from Jesus, and my accusers failed and were punished. This was a great victory and certainly had more positive results. Before I left, I found a charismatic church leader to lead the church until their next chapter. People would support me and see I had done great things. Indeed, comparing these two scenarios gives us a clear desire to strive for the second circumstance.

But what if we look deeper? What if we actually pay attention to the context in which these two situations took place? And what if we look at the actual historical accounts and the eventual results?

The first mission trip scenario was Paul's journey to what became the church at Philippi. In the epistle to the Philippians, Paul said this church was an example to others, and they brought him joy.

> I thank my God in all my remembrance of you, always in every prayer of mine for you all making my prayer with joy, because of your partnership in the gospel from the first day until now. And I am sure of this, that he who began a good work in you will bring it to completion at the day of Jesus Christ. It is right for me to feel this way about you all, because I hold you in my heart, for you are all partakers with

me of grace, both in my imprisonment and in the defense and confirmation of the gospel. (Philippians 1:3–7)

He loved this church and saw so much goodness in them. Paul's words to them exude the pride and joy of a parent who sees their child thriving. He maintained a solid relationship with them.

As for the church in the second scenario, the church of Corinth, it didn't go quite as well. They turned against him after he left and had a lot of in-fighting, later turning on each other. Paul wrote three letters telling them to straighten up and implied a threat against them if they did not. He didn't hesitate to inform them of their failures and his disappointment in their behavior.

But I, brothers, could not address you as spiritual people, but as people of the flesh, as infants in Christ. I fed you with milk, not solid food, for you were not ready for it. And even now you are not yet ready, for you are still of the flesh. For while there is jealousy and strife among you, are you not of the flesh and behaving only in a human way? For when one says, 'I follow Paul,' and another, 'I follow Apollos,' are you not being merely human?" (1 Corinthians 3:1–4)

He even shared his relief that he only baptized a few of them (1 Corinthians 1:14–16) because he didn't want to have his name attached to them. "I thank God that I baptized none of you except Crispus and Gaius, so that no one may say that you were baptized in my name. (I did baptize also the household of Stephanas. Beyond that, I do not know whether I baptized anyone else.)" (1 Corinthians 1:14–16).

These two examples show us the futility of comparison. In the natural, one of these seems much more victorious and successful than the other. We may see more glory in one circumstance compared to the other. But is that how God sees it? Is he as focused on immediate results as we are? Comparison robs you of your boldness. Results are often man-driven and not God- driven or ordained. His plan is perfect, and we don't need to understand it.

When it comes to this issue of comparison, we can easily see how all these different roadblocks can actually be interlinked. We compare based on immediacy, which stems from our idol of convenience and instant results. We compare our lack of confidence against someone else's achievements. We compare what is and isn't comfortable, such as being beaten in prison as opposed to seeing our accusers beaten instead.

We compare our commitment level to another person's, and we get cynical when we think we are less effective than they are. When it comes to all the different underlying excuses there are, we must remember that none of them can stand up against God's call on our lives to be bold.

Lastly, consider the one type of comparison we see in Scripture that is a humble and right understanding of the gospel of grace through the words of Paul in 1 Timothy 1:15–16.

> The saying is trustworthy and deserving of full acceptance, that Christ Jesus came into the world to save sinners, *of whom I am the foremost.* But I received mercy for this reason, that in me, *as the foremost,* Jesus Christ might display his perfect patience as an example to those who were to believe in him for eternal life. (emphasis added)

Paul's comparison of himself to others led him to believe he was the chiefest of sinners. He wasn't comparing his inadequacy or his faults; he wasn't letting them bring him down and make him insecure. He was giving glory to God for saving even someone like him.

This is how we should be, looking to our own selves in light of the mercy of God. That is the comparison we need to consider. Who are we according to his grace? What would we be without that grace? And is our identity found in that person or is our identity bound up in the redemption of a merciful God?

Are you comparing yourself to anyone else. Are you letting those comparisons hinder you from doing what God requires of you? Are you allowing your insecurities to stop you from obedience just because it's hard?

Whether you need to repent before God or even go to that person and ask forgiveness for how you've seen them as competition, don't waste another day holding back from boldness just because you don't think you're as (fill in the blank) as someone else. Compared to Jesus, we are all unworthy. But his grace is sufficient for even you.

The Comparison of the Proud

We might also compare ourselves with others and come out on top. This is dangerous. We compare our righteousness, strength, or wealth with those who don't have it. We start relying on our own power or self-righteousness, and this becomes an obstacle as well. Because we are relying on these qualities, we are afraid we will lose them or have to give them up.

I don't want to be like that person, we may think. But it really doesn't matter if we want to be like them or not. We are called to be exactly who God has made us to be, just as they are called to be the person He has made them to be.

When we start comparing ourselves to others, we fall into the trap of the Pharisees. Jesus warned us about this in a parable in Luke 18:9–14.

> He also told this parable to some who trusted in themselves that they were righteous, and treated others with contempt: "Two men went up into the temple to pray, one a Pharisee and the other a tax collector. The Pharisee, standing by himself, prayed thus: 'God, I thank you that I am not like other men, extortioners, unjust, adulterers, or even like this tax collector. I fast twice a week; I give tithes of all that I get.' But the tax collector, standing far off, would not even lift up his eyes to heaven, but beat his breast, saying, 'God, be merciful to me, a sinner!' I tell you, this man went down to his house justified, rather than the other. For everyone who exalts himself will be humbled, but the one who humbles himself will be exalted."

If Jesus condemns this sort of thinking, who are we to think it's acceptable? Are we so caught up in our pride that we no longer recognize our need for him?

Comparison can take root in our hearts in various forms. Whether you are feeling like you'll never be good enough to even try or that you've already achieved righteousness through your moral goodness, you're missing the point. We are called by Jesus to be bold, humbly so, just as he was. He is the example of our faith and, as such, we should seek the same bold humility he demonstrated.

None of us is so perfect that we don't need him. We must always seek him in everything. We must lean into his strength and righteousness. All else is meaningless.

For Reflection

1. In what areas of your life do you feel tempted to compare yourself with others, and how does this comparison impact your ability to act boldly? Reflect on a recent situation where comparison held you back from taking a bold step. How can you overcome this in the future?_

2. What people or situations do you find yourself comparing yourself to most frequently? How do these comparisons make you feel about your own abilities and goals?

3. Think of a time when you felt discouraged because you compared your achievements to someone else's. How did this comparison affect your motivation and actions? How could you have handled it differently to stay motivated and bold?

4. How do your insecurities about your abilities or achievements affect your willingness to be bold in pursuing what God has called you to do? What steps can you take to overcome these insecurities?

5. In what ways has social media contributed to your struggles with comparison? How can you adjust your social media habits to reduce its negative impact on your sense of self-worth and boldness?

6. How can you shift from a mindset of competing with others to one of emulating positive behaviors and attitudes? Reflect on how this shift could help you act more boldly and authentically._

7. Reflect on the two missionary scenarios provided. How does understanding the different outcomes of these missions influence your view of success and failure in your own endeavors? How can you apply these lessons to your personal or professional life?

8. How can reflecting on Paul's view of himself as the foremost of sinners help you place your identity and confidence in God's grace rather than in comparisons with others? What changes might you make in your life to align more closely with this perspective?

CHAPTER TEN:

Lack of Compassion

A lack of compassion is very similar to a lack of concern, and the circles of excuses may overlap. However, the primary difference is the lack of compassion deals with those who have harmed you while the lack of concern deals with those people whose interactions are neutral or positive toward you. With a lack of concern, it's more about prioritizing, whereas a lack of compassion tends to be a matter of negative feelings or emotions.

So what does your compassion have to do with boldness? How is compassion shown in our day-to-day interactions, and what does it mean in regard to standing firm in your faith and in the truth of the gospel?

It requires a lot of boldness to forgive those who have harmed you. It is an act of showing the grace of Jesus. We demonstrate this grace and mercy, as is often the case, through our responses to those who have harmed us. It takes a bold, strong will to let go of the type of hurts many live with, the hurts that truly bury us or cause us great pain.

But if we are determined to forgive and to obey what God has commanded of us in his Word, we will do it regardless of what it may cost. This call to forgiveness does not have anything to do with self-defense. If we are attacked, we have a right to defend ourselves or our family in that moment. We aren't commanded in Scripture to be pacifists who just allow ourselves and/or our families to be endangered without consequence. But afterward, we can still forgive the person for attacking us.

Our boldness can be inhibited by our lack of forgiveness toward others. We can either lose boldness toward that person due to the hate and anger we have built up, or we can lose boldness because our forgiveness prohibits us from listening to the Holy Spirit and allowing Him to enable or gift us the boldness necessary to complete our task.

A lack of forgiveness leads to belligerent behavior. This is why you see so many angry people screaming at others on social media and in the streets. This anger against Christians will ultimately spill out as violence.

When you are angry and you have to stand up against someone or something, then the boldness comes across emotionally. This emotion allows you to lose control, resulting in belligerent behavior.

Forgiveness helps you, not them. It is mentioned in the Bible numerous times, and whenever God's forgives us, it is always conditional on our forgiveness of others.

The Lord's Prayer asks God to forgive us *as* we forgive others. "Forgive us our debts, as we also have forgiven our debtors" (Matthew 6:14). We also see this same principle clearly illustrated in the parable of the unforgiving servant, found in Matthew 18. We see a man who has been forgiven much, but he cannot forgive even a little.

> Then Peter came up and said to him, "Lord, how often will my brother sin against me, and I forgive him? As many as seven times?" Jesus said to him, "I do not say to you seven times, but seventy-seven times.
>
> "Therefore the kingdom of heaven may be compared to a king who wished to settle accounts with his servants. When he began to settle, one was brought to him who owed him ten thousand talents. And since he could not pay, his master ordered him to be sold, with his wife and children and all that he had, and payment to be made. So the servant fell on his knees, imploring him, 'Have patience with me, and I will pay you everything.' And out of pity for him, the master of that servant released him and forgave him the debt. But when that same servant went out, he found one of

his fellow servants who owed him a hundred denarii, and seizing him, he began to choke him, saying, 'Pay what you owe.' So his fellow servant fell down and pleaded with him, 'Have patience with me, and I will pay you.' He refused and went and put him in prison until he should pay the debt. When his fellow servants saw what had taken place, they were greatly distressed, and they went and reported to their master all that had taken place. Then his master summoned him and said to him, 'You wicked servant! I forgave you all that debt because you pleaded with me. And should not you have had mercy on your fellow servant, as I had mercy on you?' And in anger his master delivered him to the jailers, until he should pay all his debt. So also my heavenly Father will do to every one of you, if you do not forgive your brother from your heart.'"

We often think that we do mostly good things and don't need to be forgiven for much. Maybe we weren't nice to someone in middle school, and we still feel bad about it. Maybe a more serious incident happened in our past, and we were unfaithful to a spouse, or we caused a tragedy by running a red light.

But are these the debts we owe? Must we seek forgiveness for these? Or is it that we need God's continual grace, mercy, and compassion for each and every little sin that has ever crept into our hearts? Do we need to offer restitution for big mistakes, or are we humbling enough to see that a single act of uninhibited wickedness is enough to condemn us to hell? Can we acknowledge that our moment of pride, our unrighteous anger, or even our lack of forgiveness toward another is enough to separate us from a holy God, and only by his sacrifice can we approach him?

Forgiveness is not conditional on the other person. We are to give forgiveness regardless of what the other person does. Even if they have never apologized for the awful thing they did to us, we are called to forgive. Even if they caused the tragedy in our life by running that red light. Even if they are the unfaithful spouse. Even if they were cruel to us in middle school when we were at our least secure in our identity.

We are called to forgive. We are called to look at the mercy God has shown us, and we offer that forgiveness in turn. Not just for their sake but for our own. If we cling to the pain, we will never have peace.

In the previous passage in Matthew 18, Jesus tells Peter that even if we are sinned against seven times, then we forgive when they ask. Can you imagine intentionally being punched or gossiped about seven times a day? That's one time every three and half hours. This would not be easy even if the offender were your closest friend or family member. But Jesus actually said seventy times seven, and if you are truly forgiving someone, the 490th time you forgive them is the first time.[55]

When we can show people we forgive them, it takes strength, but it also points people to Jesus and allows us opportunities to share the gospel. We can demonstrate his love through forgiveness, even if the other person scoffs or laughs it off, thinking it's worthless.

Some may collapse into tears, grateful for your forgiveness. They may be touched in their hearts by your willingness to let go of what they've done. Or they may be callous and think their actions didn't matter. They may think you're being foolish for being hurt in the first place. Sometimes that response requires even more patience and forgiveness from you. Now you have to forgive not only the initial act but the callous response of someone who doesn't even feel bad about it. Still, you are called to forgive. Still, you are called to gratitude for the mercy God has shown you and to be guided by that.

When others find out about our forgiveness, they truly may not understand. That's okay. It's totally fine if they don't get it at first. We still need to act and forgive, and it will help people learn more about who Jesus is and the power he has in our lives. That is our calling and purpose.

Forgiveness is an incredible evangelism tool. Their lack of compassion may have hurt, but it doesn't have to linger. It doesn't have to be our ending. Forgiveness can be the beginning of a new life for them and an act of boldness for you.

It's truly in your hands.

---

[55] To be perfectly clear, we are discussing forgiveness. This differs from setting boundaries, and forgiveness does not mean enabling. Of course, place boundaries where appropriate and don't enable someone's poor treatment of you. Get out of bad situations or areas where you may be in danger. I'm not encouraging you to be a doormat. In many ways today, forgiveness is also being redefined to mean these other things, but I'm referencing the biblical wisdom of forgiveness and honoring God by showing grace and mercy to those who have hurt us while maintaining boldness.

Pastor Allen Jackson, when discussing the previous election season, shared a valuable analogy.[56]

> If you go to the doctor for a physical . . . on an annual basis, or whatever your particular circumstances are, for a health evaluation, they'll draw blood and they'll do some lab work on you, and they'll come back and talk to you about your cholesterol levels, too low or too high, or your sugar levels being too low or too high, or your triglycerides. It's an evaluation of how you are at that level. They may take a chest x-ray and look at your lungs, or if you're really fortunate, they'll give you an EKG, and if you just hit the double lotto winner, you get to do a treadmill test. And then they'll stand there and you're all hooked up, and they will make you exercise until you fail—with kind of a smirk on their faces while they're doing it.
>
> And when you're done with all of that, they're going to give you an evaluation on your health. Tell you how to adjust your diet, or increase your exercise, or change your routines, or if there's some intervention that might be necessary, what that would look like. But the fundamental nature of that arrangement—understand that the doctor's visit does not make you healthier. You don't walk out of the doctor's office going, "Whoa, I needed that." It's an evaluation, it's to provide awareness so that you could adapt your behavior to improve your physical health. Don't bring as many fork folds to your mouth and move more. And I'm going to weigh you again in 12 months to see how you've done with that.
>
> Now, you can blame McDonald's, or processed food, but ultimately it's usually our hands that move it towards your mouth. I mean, doctors can provide some awareness of previously unacknowledged problems, but the outcomes are more in your arena than theirs.

While Pastor Allen Jackson uses this analogy for election results and how we respond to them, this is an extremely valuable analogy

---

[56] "Allen Jackson - disaster, disappointment, and hope - part 1," Sermons.love, accessed May 16, 2025, https://sermons.love/allen-jackson/13304-allen-jackson-disaster-disappointment-and-hope-part-1.html.

when dealing with our own forgiveness of others.

Forgiveness is about our own spiritual health, and we determine whether or not we are going to be healthy. Holding onto our penchant for anger or bitterness against those who hurt us will only cause us further disease. It may be a sickness in our hearts, where we simply cave to the rage inside us and we can't see how we have been forgiven. Or maybe our anger will come out physically in the form of high blood pressure or burnout because we are so stuck in our negative emotions.

But ultimately, it's in our hands. We can go to God for our evaluation, but how we respond is up to us. We can ask him for wisdom as to how to proceed. We would ask a doctor how we can lower our blood sugar naturally and without medication, and he would tell us to decrease our carb intake or get more exercise. In the same way, the Holy Spirit provides wisdom as to how to let go of the hurts from others so we can have freedom to love others and to forgive them despite what they have done.

Use this tool of evangelism for the benefits it provides. Demonstrate the truth and beauty of God's forgiveness by emulating that here on earth. You never know whose bucket needs a few drops of forgiveness before it's ready to overflow.

Forgiveness does not mean we don't set boundaries. We can forgive but still not have to be around those who hurt us. David forgave Saul. He would not kill him when he had the chance to do so in spite of being hunted by Saul. Even when he cut off Saul's robe, David felt guilty for doing so. When questioned by others, David said he would not touch the Lord's anointed. Yet he no longer hung out in the castle playing the harp. He ran and hid. But he still forgave.

The Flip Side

Before we move on, let's consider the reverse. What if you were lacking in compassion? Maybe someone you disliked did something that hurt you (leading to a lack of forgiveness) or maybe you just have a mean streak like some people do. If you simply don't like a particular person, you may not get overly excited by the idea of sharing eternity with them.

Truthfully, we will probably be sharing eternity with many people even though we don't particularly enjoy having to see them for even five minutes here on earth. It could be that weird lady at church who's a bit manipulative or maybe that underperforming employee who's always awkwardly hinting that he wants a raise even though he's only been on the job for two months.

Whatever the case may be, some of these people will be in heaven with us in the end. But what about those who aren't currently on the narrow path? Do you have compassion for them? Even if they are the worst person you know, do you desire to see them come to know Christ? Will you be heartbroken over their lost souls? Are you bold enough to pray for them and to choose compassion when you may not want to?

We have to ask ourselves these questions. It's challenging to seek their interests when we dislike them so much, but we are called to pray for our enemies and love our neighbors. Resist the urge to let your dislike of someone overwhelm your desire to see the lost finally found. Have compassion on those who are so hard to love.

You never know how God will use you with those people. It could be, yet again, that your testimony of loving them compassionately, despite your actual dislike for them, will turn their hearts around and help them seek God for the first time in their lives. It's worth praying about and seeking God for boldness. You just have to make a choice. Are you going to continue in disdain, or will you choose compassion?

For Reflection

1. Think about someone who has harmed you in the past. Consider any lingering bitterness. How do you feel about that person now? Do you still hold onto feelings of anger or resentment toward them? How does holding onto these feelings impact your relationship with that person and your own peace?

2. Have you truly forgiven someone who has wronged you, or do you find yourself revisiting the offense and feeling bitterness when you think about them? Reflect on your forgiveness process. Are there areas where you still need to fully forgive someone, or where bitterness lingers?

3. How do you usually react when someone close to you makes a mistake or fails to meet your expectations? How can you practice more patience and grace in these situations?

4. Reflect on your empathy toward others. When you see someone struggling or in pain, do you find yourself wanting to help and alleviate their suffering, or do you tend to feel indifferent or dismissive? How can you cultivate a deeper desire to help those in need, especially when they are struggling?

5. Can you forgive someone who has wronged you while still setting appropriate boundaries to protect yourself from further harm? How do you distinguish between forgiveness and enabling? How can you forgive while maintaining healthy boundaries?

6. Can you pray for those who have hurt you or whom you dislike? Do you find it challenging to ask God to bless them or to seek their well-being? How does this challenge your understanding of forgiveness and compassion?

7. How do you feel about people who are difficult to love or who might have caused you discomfort? How can you learn to see them through the eyes of compassion rather than judgment?

8. When someone criticizes you or challenges your beliefs, do

you respond with patience and understanding, or do you react defensively and with hostility? Think about how you respond to criticism. How can you grow in responding with patience and grace, rather than defensiveness?

9. Are you motivated to share the gospel with those who might be hard to reach or who have shown hostility toward your faith? How does compassion influence your approach to evangelism? How can you approach difficult situations with a heart for sharing the gospel?

10. Do you regularly reflect on your own need for forgiveness and grace? Are you mindful of how your own actions might fall short and how much you rely on God's compassion for yourself? How does acknowledging your need for forgiveness help you extend that same grace to others?

CHAPTER ELEVEN

Fear of Conflict

We've looked at a number of responses I receive from people when they're challenged to be bold. Some of these may have been familiar to you, and some may have seemed unusual or unexpected. But I often hear these and can't ignore them because these are really just excuses to justify disobedience. At the end of the day, none of us can really say these reasons are more important than honoring the Word of God. But people use even more excuses, so we'll look at a couple of others before we move on to the solutions.

A very popular response I get from people who hesitate in their boldness is the anticipation people will be mad at them. They are afraid of offending someone, so they don't want to say anything at all. Many of us can probably relate to this concern, and so many of the Christians who stay quiet seem to do so because they don't know what the consequences may look like if they do speak up.

This is very closely related to the lack of comfort we may feel when we're asked to step out in faith when it's hard. One cannot have a fear of conflict without a lack of comfort, but one can have a lack of comfort without the fear of conflict. It really just depends on the source of the struggle and where their heart is on this particular issue.

In campus videos from different conservative platforms, like

Turning Point USA or Students for Life, they will sometimes ask a question of a progressive student that traps them. They'll ask questions such as whether or not women should be given the choice to abort a child and when the student answers that she should, they then ask what constitutes a woman to begin with. Or they will ask if white men have benefits they don't have, and the female minority student will say yes, but when they're asked what those benefits are, the student may not be able to answer.

You see the fear of conflict in these students' eyes. They have been trapped by their own logic, and now they can't get out of it without giving the wrong answer. After all, how can a woman have the right to abortion if it's wrong to define gender? How can we stand firm with DEI policies if we don't actually know how we're being oppressed?

But just as we see this fear of conflict in those students, we see a similar fear of conflict in many Christians. We will be asked if something is a sin, and then, returning to the idea of redefining terms, we will be reminded that judging is sinful. No matter what, our response will bring conflict. If we respond from a lack of knowledge of the real context, we will stumble through an uninformed answer. If we understand judgment biblically and answer accordingly, we will have a deeper argument on our hands as both parties are using the word judgment to mean two totally different things. I used to do this when I was not a Christian, and as a predator, I could easily spot prey. When I found someone who was bold or willing to stand, I generally avoided them.

Most people don't enjoy conflict although, to be fair, some people out there truly enjoy it. But for many, it's a nightmare, and it gets their hearts racing until they feel sick. It's a challenge they avoid because no one wants to think they are upsetting other people due to their own opinions. Opinions and truth are two separate things, and we shouldn't argue from opinion but from truth. And even then, the argument should be based in love and humility—but also in boldness.

We may think, I could not be bold because someone might be mad at me, but sometimes they have nothing to do with my life at all. It could be the person at the convenience store or a protester. You might never see that person again, and you have to choose whether to plant a seed or to cower. Also, people don't worry about making others angry when it comes to their favorite sports team or restaurant. We have no issue saying, "My team is better," or "I don't like where you choose to eat."

Of course, you need to use judgment and wisdom to know how to respond to people in these situations, especially if you don't know them. Their background has possibly led them down this path, and you simply don't have the opportunity to unpack that. All the more reason to show them grace as you approach your conversation boldly.

We often fear people's response to us. We judge that fear based on the looks someone gives us or an outright screaming match that may happen. On some level, I think the looks are harder to deal with because we assume the worst since we don't know exactly what they're thinking. Instead, we just project what we assume to be their thoughts—which is often far uglier than the reality. We don't know if it is disappointment, if we were wrong, if we lost a friend, etc.

When someone screams at us, we can easily become angry or justify their actions by labeling them as crazy. We can allow our self-righteousness to then justify why we are bold. This is not a correct perspective, but let's be honest and admit that it is much easier to be self-righteous than to rely on the righteousness of Jesus that has been given to us.

So what if they get angry with you? What if there is mild or moderate conflict? So what?[57] What harm does that do compared to the potential harm of not being bold? A person can be angry, or they can go to hell. Is your responsibility to keep them happy, or is it to share the gospel? (Matthew 28:18–20). I am not saying that they will certainly go to Hell if you do or don't stand boldly, but what part would you play in showing them Christ if you did choose to speak up as opposed to staying silent?

Jesus says we should not fear those that can harm us physically. "Do not be afraid of those who kill the body but cannot kill the soul. Rather, be afraid of the One who can destroy both soul and body in hell" (Matthew 10:28).

---

[57] We never want to ask what difference it makes out of cynicism as previously discussed. But to ask "so what?" out of obedience and boldness is a totally different question and circumstance. This is a time to truly look at the value of following what God has commanded instead of being distracted by someone's potential anger.

Furthermore, by fearing others and avoiding this conflict, we go against the very truth of what Jesus said. He tells us there will be conflict. He said family will leave and that people will persecute you. If we are going to trust his words, we have to be prepared for this. And when it inevitably happens, we can't view ourselves as victims of it. We have to continue pursuing his call on our lives.

> Then he said to them, "Nation will rise against nation, and kingdom against kingdom. There will be great earthquakes, and in various places famines and pestilences. And there will be terrors and great signs from heaven. But before all this they will lay their hands on you and persecute you, delivering you up to the synagogues and prisons, and you will be brought before kings and governors for my name's sake. This will be your opportunity to bear witness. Settle it therefore in your minds not to meditate beforehand how to answer, for I will give you a mouth and wisdom, which none of your adversaries will be able to withstand or contradict. You will be delivered up even by parents and brothers and relatives and friends, and some of you they will put to death. You will be hated by all for my name's sake. But not a hair of your head will perish. By your endurance you will gain your lives." (Luke 21:10–19)

When you try to avoid what Jesus is telling you will happen, it means you have to go against his will. To do his will means you will have conflict, whether you like it or not. But the Bible gives us plenty of other promises about conflict and persecution. We have to bear these in mind as well because they show us just how worthwhile it is to endure the discomfort.

Are you willing to go through temporary pain for the sake of the gospel? Is the work of Christ on the cross valuable enough that you would give up today for the sake of eternity with him? Here's what his Word has to say on the matter:

> Bless those who persecute you; bless and do not curse them. Rejoice with those who rejoice, weep with those who weep. Live in harmony with one another. Do not be haughty, but associate with the lowly. Never be wise in your own sight.

Repay no one evil for evil, but give thought to do what is honorable in the sight of all. If possible, so far as it depends on you, live peaceably with all. Beloved, never avenge yourselves, but leave it to the wrath of God, for it is written, 'Vengeance is mine, I will repay, says the Lord.' To the contrary, 'if your enemy is hungry, feed him; if he is thirsty, give him something to drink; for by so doing you will heap burning coals on his head.' Do not be overcome by evil, but overcome evil with good." (Romans 12:14–21)

Blessed are those who are persecuted for righteousness' sake, for theirs is the kingdom of heaven.

Blessed are you when others revile you and persecute you and utter all kinds of evil against you falsely on my account. Rejoice and be glad, for your reward is great in heaven, for so they persecuted the prophets who were before you. (Matthew 5:10–12)

Again, what would you prefer? Do you only want to avoid the persecution that we have been promised? Surely, you can try. But you can't try without making significant compromises of the faith and giving up the truth. Or would you prefer to face the fact that you will struggle in this world and live in obedience to Christ so that you will have a beautiful eternity with him?

Jesus also tells us we will be hated because the world hates him (John 15:18–19). Would we rather be on the side of the world or be hated for our reverence for Christ? Would we rather suffer with him now or suffer for all eternity, separated from him?

We have to consider these consequences when we're lacking in boldness simply because of a fear of conflict. We can't pretend our fear of conflict means nothing when, in reality, it determines a major aspect of how we live.

The fact we have to acknowledge is the gospel is divisive. Jesus warned he didn't come to bring peace to the world (Matthew 10:34–36). He came because he is the Savior of the world, but not everyone wants to be saved. He came to bring a very clear distinction between the redeemed and the wicked. He came so that those whom he called would know Him while the others would be cast aside.

If we are going to live like Jesus and ask what would Jesus do, then we also have to stand like Jesus stood. Again, we do it with humility and love, not with belligerence, but this requires that we get out of our comfort zones, accept that conflict will occur, and celebrate truth. We don't shirk away because it may cost us something. We don't stay silent because we're afraid of offending someone.

The gospel is offensive. The gospel requires that people acknowledge their imperfections and accept the label of sinner. That's not easy for anyone. But it is a requirement of salvation. We can't be sanctified or even justified without repentance, and we can't repent without admitting our sin. That's going to offend people. And that's perfectly okay if it means that they might come to know God as a result.

While the belligerent find a bit of pleasure out of trapping and offending others for their religious or moral views, the bold speak out of courage and a passion for truth. They seek to wake others to the grace and mercy of Jesus, even when it's hard. Who are you afraid of offending? Who in your life needs to know about Jesus, but you can't quite bring yourself to have that difficult conversation?

Pray today for boldness, wisdom, and the ability to step away from the fear of conflict and find the words to share the truth. Be ready for the fact that conflict may come anyway. That's okay. Let this person know how much you love and care for them and that you aren't trying to offend them, but you understand the gospel can be offensive. Show them you care for their eternity and that you speak the truth out of love.

If we let the Holy Spirit guide us, we don't need to worry about belligerence. Others may interpret our boldness that way, even if we aren't doing anything to contribute to it, but we can't do anything about their response. That's up to the Holy Spirit. Only he can turn a heart of stone into a heart of flesh. Your job isn't to save anyone; it's to boldly proclaim the Word of God and to love others enough to be honest about the truth—even if it ends in conflict.

For Reflection

1. How do you typically respond when someone challenges your beliefs or opinions? Do you avoid the conversation, become defensive, engage with them openly, or something else?

2. Have you ever held back from sharing your faith or expressing a biblical viewpoint because you feared the potential reaction of others? What fear or concern caused you to hold back, and how might you overcome it next time?

3. When faced with a situation where speaking the truth might lead to conflict, how do you weigh the potential for discomfort against the importance of the message you want to convey? Do you prioritize peace over truth, or do you stand firm in your beliefs even at the risk of conflict?

4. Can you recall a time when you chose not to address a moral or spiritual issue in a conversation because you were concerned it might upset the other person? What was the outcome of that decision? How did that choice impact the situation or your relationship with that person?

5. How do you deal with negative reactions or hostility when you express your beliefs? Do you remain steadfast in your beliefs, or are you more likely to back down to avoid confrontation?

6. In your daily interactions, how comfortable are you with disagreement or differing opinions? Do you find yourself compromising your views to maintain harmony? Are you willing to respectfully disagree, or do you feel the need to conform to maintain peace?

7. How do you handle situations when others might perceive the truth you believe in as offensive? How do you balance speaking the truth with maintaining peace?

8. Do you actively seek to understand the perspectives of those who disagree with you, or do you avoid these discussions to prevent

potential conflict? How can you engage with people who disagree with you in a way that fosters respect and understanding?

9. How do you reconcile the call to live peacefully with others (Romans 12:18) with the reality that speaking the gospel may inevitably cause division (Matthew 10:34–36)?

10. Reflect on your prayer life: Do you pray for boldness, wisdom, and strength to stand firm in your beliefs in a way that honors God, or do you seek comfort and peace above all else?

Chapter Twelve

Lack of Control

The first time I took my son horseback riding, we made sure to tell him he had to stay in control of the horse. Despite being a small boy on a much larger horse, Jamey was determined to handle the horse. As we were on the trail, the horse suddenly broke into a trot, and Jamey's feet flew out of the stirrups, his legs flapping against the horse's sides. His hands were struggling to hold the reins steady. In the midst of this chaos, Jamey's voice was filled with fear as he kept shouting, "I am in control! I am in control!"

I understand Jamey's determination to declare his control in the midst of that moment. That may be how we feel, but the reality is that we have no control. Just because we want control or know that we *need* it in the moment doesn't mean that like Jamey, we actually have it or that we can handle the circumstances we've been given. We still think we have control even as everything is spinning around us.

That's why this is such an important topic. The last obstacle we often face is that we don't want to give up on control—whether or not we actually have it. We lack boldness because we see ourselves as a server wanting a tip from God rather than as a servant who lives in obedience to the Lord, our Christ. We expect to have some power in this relationship as opposed to completely abandoning our own will for the sake of his sovereign will. We place our trust in our own hands when they are weak and incapable of actually doing much of anything.

When we see a tit-for-tat relationship with God, we feel we have no reason to be bold. We expect something in return, and then we miss out on the opportunity to be bold. If we can't see the benefit of our boldness, then we simply won't be bold. It's a false mindset and a poor judgment of what it is to live according to the truth. After all, do we really think God needs our help to lead us? Or are we willing to place all our faith and trust in his hands?

We have to remember who God is and who we are in relation to him. If we see him rightly, as the God and Creator of all things, as the righteous Judge, and as the sovereign Ruler, we can more easily understand our lack of control. We can also more easily accept and let go of what little control we think we have.

But who is God in light of control? What does the Bible say about his power?

> I form light and create darkness;
>   I make well-being and create calamity;
>   I am the Lord, who does all these things.
> "Shower, O heavens, from above,
>   and let the clouds rain down righteousness;
>   let the earth open, that salvation and righteousness may
>   bear fruit;
>   let the earth cause them both to sprout;
>   I the Lord have created it.
> Woe to him who strives with him who formed him,
>   a pot among earthen pots!
>   Does the clay say to him who forms it, "What are you
>   making?"
>   or "Your work has no handles?" (Isaiah 45:7–9)

We expect a return on our investment for our holiness and righteousness. This is the wrong attitude. What we have to understand is our obedience to God is not done for a reward. Quite the contrary, we are rewarded because of the grace of God through Jesus's sacrifice. Our obedience is the result of the mercy we have already been shown.

Still, even when we know this in our heads, often, our hearts will deceive us and lead us to believe that we choose to do the right things, and we receive blessings as a result. This is a false gospel no different from the prosperity gospel or any other give-and-receive interpretations of Scripture that take verses out of context.

But there's more to it than that. This mentality implies we have control—or that we at least share control. We may give lip service to this power, but the reality is that God alone is in control.

So often, we act the same way as when we give someone the remote to the TV. We hand it over but then tell them what channel to turn to. We do this with God. We say he is in control, but then we expect him to follow our lead and tell him the outcome we want. Ultimately, in our small frame of mind, we get upset when he doesn't listen and instead continues to lead us a different way.

The reason we so often can't let go and serve God as servants is because we don't want to give up the control required to serve God as our Lord. Somehow, we believe we have a better idea of what we need and what control should be over our lives, despite all evidence to the contrary.

When we choose a path contrary to where we know God wants to lead us, it always turns out for the worse. Ignoring that still, small voice is a recipe for hardship. And while God can use even our disobedience for good, we often have to learn hard lessons through the process.

Such beauty is available to us when we surrender our need for control and accept his will for our lives.

> In him we have obtained an inheritance, having been predestined according to the purpose of him who works all things according to the counsel of his will, so that we who were the first to hope in Christ might be to the praise of his glory. In him you also, when you heard the word of truth, the gospel of your salvation, and believed in him, were sealed with the promised Holy Spirit, who is the guarantee of our inheritance until we acquire possession of it, to the praise of his glory. (Ephesians 1:11–14)

How marvelous this is! How incredible it is to know that by giving up our need for control, we can live in the counsel of his will and obtain the inheritance of salvation. This is an amazing gift, but it's a gift we are all too willing to hold in one hand, all the while fighting his will with the other hand. But to be bold when it's hard, to let go of the control when we don't want to, that is what God has called us to.

Our boldness requires us to give up control and that is part of what makes it so challenging. Our boldness could put all of the following in jeopardy, our friendships, our jobs, our freedom, and even our lives. We have to accept our need for control isn't just the idea of wanting to buy a car but feeling that still, small voice telling me it's not wise to go that deep into debt. In some areas, we need to exercise wisdom and obedience, but at times, letting go of control and being bold really can lead to dire consequences.

Still, the Bible leads us in remembering where our trust lies. We are consistently reminded that we should certainly be paying attention, that we are seeking the eternal.

> So have no fear of them, for nothing is covered that will not be revealed, or hidden that will not be known. What I tell you in the dark, say in the light, and what you hear whispered, proclaim on the housetops. And do not fear those who kill the body but cannot kill the soul. Rather fear him who can destroy both soul and body in hell. Are not two sparrows sold for a penny? And not one of them will fall to the ground apart from your Father. But even the hairs of your head are all numbered. Fear not, therefore; you are of more value than many sparrows. So everyone who acknowledges me before men, I also will acknowledge before my Father who is in heaven, but whoever denies me before men, I also will deny before my Father who is in heaven. (Matthew 10:26–33)

When we consider the apostles and other followers of Jesus, we realize what they gave up. What were the consequences of their boldness? History and Scripture tell us what happened to some of those prominent, early followers of Christ.

These men followed Jesus as disciples and members of the early church. They helped birth and lead it. They were bold and went against the powers of the time. Rather than cling to their need for control and comfort, they abandoned everything for the will of God. Let's look at how the lives of these men ended:

- Peter—Crucified
- James—Beheaded
- Thomas—Murdered in India
- Paul—Beheaded
- John—Left to die on an island
- Andrew—Crucified
- Phillip—Put to death by a Roman proconsul
- Matthew—There is some doubt about his death, but some believe he was stabbed to death in Ethiopia
- Bartholomew—Killed but it is unclear as to how. Some think he was flayed alive, and others think he was beheaded
- James—Martyred—unclear how
- Simon—Killed after refusing to worship the sun god
- Matthias—Burned to death
- Stephen—Stoned to death[58]

When these men were faced with the choice of boldness or of trying to control their own outcomes, they gave up their own wills entirely to follow the will of God.[59]

Judas was the only disciple that showed a lack of boldness. As a result, he was filled with regret and remorse and killed himself. Judas tried to be in control and gave in to the crowd. It didn't go well (Revelation 21:8).

Different personality types may struggle more than others when it comes to the issue of control. Regardless of whether or not you're the list-obsessed, every-moment planner, or the laid-back, go-with-the-flow wanderer, it all comes down to a matter of trust.

---

[58] Ken Curtis, PhD, "What Happened to the Twelve Apostles and How Did They Die?," December 10, 2024, Christianity, https://www.christianity.com/church/church-history/timeline/1-300/whatever-happened-to-the-twelve-apostles-11629558.html.

[59] Sometimes humor wakes us up to reality in a way that logic can't. To look at the cost of the boldness of these men from a different perspective, the video "If Jesus' Resurrection Were a Hoax" from *The Babylon Bee* helps us recognize that no one would ever go through what they went through unless they were fully surrendered to the will of God. The Babylon Bee, "If Jesus' Resurrection Were A Hoax," March 30, 2023, YouTube, https://www.youtube.com/watch?v=23UNLLbOS3w.

Where do you put your trust? Is it in your own plans and dreams, or is it placed on the firm foundation of Christ alone?

Control and faith can either complement one another, or they can be purely antithetical, depending on how they're handled. When placed in the right hands, our faith will be our strongest source of life.

We don't need to fear the lack of control just because it's out of our hands. The truth is that it was never in our hands. It has always been by the grace of God alone that we wake up in the morning, that we have a roof over our heads, that we have a morsel to eat.

In my interview with Reverend Kevin McGary for my podcast, Kevin makes it very simple. We cannot even control the next breath we take. No one can do that, which places our entire lives in the hands of God—the one who truly determines the next breath we take. And by the grace of God, those who place their trust in Christ will one day not wake up in the morning. On that day, we will stand before him without sorrow or pain.

What is the absolute worst thing we can imagine happening to us if we let go of our perception of control? We may think God won't provide, that we'll lose our house, or that the economy will crash due to poor leadership.

But biblically, these are not the worst things that can happen. The worst thing that ever happened to anyone in history was to be separated from God. When God the Son died on the cross, he was forsaken by God the Father. Romans 8:31–39 assures us this will never happen to us.

> What then shall we say to these things? If God is for us, who can be against us? He who did not spare his own Son but gave him up for us all, how will he not also with him graciously give us all things? Who shall bring any charge against God's elect? It is God who justifies. Who is to condemn? Christ Jesus is the one who died—more than that, who was raised—who is at the right hand of God, who indeed is interceding for us. Who shall separate us from the love of Christ? Shall tribulation, or distress, or persecution, or famine, or nakedness, or danger, or sword? As it is written,
> 'For your sake we are being killed all the day long; we are regarded as sheep to be slaughtered.'

No, in all these things we are more than conquerors through him who loved us. For I am sure that neither death nor life, nor angels nor rulers, nor things present nor things to come, nor powers, nor height nor depth, nor anything else in all creation, will be able to separate us from the love of God in Christ Jesus our Lord.

Nothing will separate us. He, himself, was separated so that we would never have to endure that sort of pain. So when we place our need for control in his hands, we can rest assured he will lead us in the best way possible.

For Reflection

1. Can you recall a time when you tried to take control of a situation, only to realize you had no control? How did it affect your trust in God? Reflect on how letting go of control might deepen your dependence on Him and strengthen your faith.

2. In which areas of your life are you still trying to control outcomes, even when it's beyond your power? How does this impact your trust in God's sovereignty? Reflect on how releasing control in these areas could deepen your relationship with him.

3. How does the need to control situations hinder your boldness in living out your faith? In which areas of your life can you surrender control to God in order to take more risks for His kingdom?

4. How are fear and control intertwined in your life? In which situations do you fear letting go of control, and how can you overcome that fear by trusting God more fully? How can you learn to trust God's sovereignty in those situations, letting go of fear and embracing faith?

5. How does understanding God's complete sovereignty help you release your need to control? Reflect on Isaiah 45:7–9 and on the peace and freedom this brings to your faith.

6. How do the early disciples' sacrifices challenge you to live boldly for Christ, even when risks are involved? How might you respond to God's call to be bold, even when it involves personal cost?

7. Reflect on the tragic end of Judas compared to the boldness of the other disciples. How can you avoid making similar mistakes by trusting God's plan rather than trying to control your own fate?

8. What specific area of your life do you feel called to surrender control over to God right now? What might be holding you back from doing so? Reflect on the trust you are learning to place in God's

plan and timing.

9. How does the fear of losing control—whether it's control over your life, job, health, or relationships—keep you from trusting God's provision? How can you cling to His promises, knowing He is faithful to provide and care for you in every circumstance?

CHAPTER THIRTEEN

Reflection

Having gone through some of the primary excuses people use to not be bold, let's reexamine each of these obstacles.

Name the top three obstacles you struggle with the most. Think about this in the context of your last week and then think about it in the context of your life. It's valuable to take the time to analyze just how these fears impact your day-to-day life and how you might grow in boldness.

Lack of Comfort

Are you afraid of losing your relationships?
What has comfort stopped you from doing in the past week?
What has it stopped you from doing throughout your life?

Lack of Commitment

Do you not care about being bold enough to get involved?
Would you rather enjoy time on the beach or at a sporting event?
Do you find that you are too busy to be bold?
What has a lack of commitment stopped you from doing in the past week?

What has it stopped you from doing in the past?

Lack of Convenience

Do you spend much time without distractions listening to God?

What has the lack of convenience stopped you from doing in the past week?

What has it stopped you from doing throughout your life?

Lack of Confidence

How confident in the Bible are you?

Will you allow people to ask you questions about the Bible?

Do you spend time reading your Bible systematically?

What has a lack of confidence stopped you from doing in the past week?

What has it stopped you from doing throughout your life?

If applicable, have you taught your kids how to defend their faith? (It's not enough to just have faith.)

Lack of Consciousness

Do you spend much time looking at current events and analyzing them in the face of the Bible?

What has a lack of consciousness stopped you from doing in the past week?

What has it stopped you from doing throughout your life?

Cynical

Do you find yourself in a position where you do not pray for people or yourself because you think it will do no good or that it is too late?

Do you measure success by the results or the process?

What has cynicism stopped you from doing in the past week?

What has it stopped you from doing throughout your life?

Comparison

Do you think you are better than other sinners you see around you?

Do you justify your actions by thinking that your sin is not as bad as their sin?

Do you think you cannot achieve the results others around you have?

What has comparison stopped you from doing in the past week?

What has it stopped you from doing throughout your life?

Compassion

When you think about people in your life, who makes you the angriest?

Have you forgiven them?

What has a lack of compassion stopped you from doing in the past week?

What has it stopped you from doing throughout your life?

Conflict

Are you considered a people pleaser?

When was the last time you made someone angry over a righteous topic?

When was the last time you made someone angry over a worldly topic?

Do you generally avoid confronting others?

What has conflict stopped you from doing in the past week?

What has it stopped you from doing throughout your life?

Control

Do you pray for prosperity?

Do you think you should be rewarded because you are better than others?

Do you live in fear?

What has control stopped you from doing in the past week?

What has it stopped you from doing throughout your life?

Your Struggles

What top three things do you struggle with the most?

What do you want to change?

Now that you know that you have a duty to be bold, if your answer is nothing, then it begs the question, why are you a Christian?

What is the number one thing you will do to fix this during the next week?

It's hard to accept the failures we carry and to repent for the issues we carry (more on that later). Still, the value of reflecting on these issues cannot be overstated. We won't ever learn how to grow in faith and boldness if we aren't willing to recognize our mistakes and make a true change.

CHAPTER FOURTEEN

Techniques for Growing Bold

After reflecting on these obstacles, many techniques can help you grow bolder, both specifically and generally. Obviously, these are not all the techniques, but they are critical for all Christians.

Some Christians utilize these strategies very consistently. Others are very inconsistent. It's important we follow these basic techniques as we start our journeys to being bold. It doesn't matter where you are in your journey—we all need to improve and grow more in our faith.

The Bible tells us how important it is to be built up in our faith and as a means of living in Christ. The problem is that if we're not reading the Bible, we won't know just how important it is to know Scripture and to be taught by it. But if we are going to grow bold and to live according to the will of Jesus, we have to be aware of what the Bible tells us.

> Therefore, as you received Christ Jesus the Lord, so walk in him, rooted and built up in him and established in the faith, just as you were taught, abounding in thanksgiving.

> See to it that no one takes you captive by philosophy
> and empty deceit, according to human tradition, according
> to the elemental spirits of the world, and not according to
> Christ. For in him the whole fullness of deity dwells bodily,
> and you have been filled in him, who is the head of all rule
> and authority. (Colossians 2:6–10)

The problem is that there is a level of being uncomfortable as we grow. Spiritual growth is like physical growth. When you work out in order to grow in health or simply to grow your muscles, it's never easy when you start. It is hard. Your muscles seem like they'll give out, and sometimes they do. Your heart rate increases, and it can be hard to breathe.

Then, the following day, your muscles are sore. The harder you work out, the sorer you become. If you continue working out with the same weight or at the same pace, it becomes much easier. After a while, your muscles don't get sore, and you can easily maintain the discipline and pace you've been exerting. You have grown to a level of ease.

But typically, it doesn't stop there. If you increase your weight or pace, you will again experience the same symptoms you had when you started. You are pushing yourself, and it becomes uncomfortable again, so you then grow some more. You have to find that discipline and consistency if you're planning to maintain the level you've been working at.

Even if you take a couple of weeks off, you will find you lose the ability to easily lift the same weight or reach the same pace as before. Without discipline, you will soon find yourself sore again.

Faith acts are not much different. If you continue doing the same thing at the same rate, you will grow stagnant. You will stop growing, but you feel like you are doing a lot. You may show up to the gym and workout, but you won't grow if you don't push yourself.

We are warned in the Bible that the Scriptures can be twisted, and if we're not cautious about growing in our understanding and our faith, we may fall into this same trap.

> Therefore, beloved, since you are waiting for these, be
> diligent to be found by him without spot or blemish, and at
> peace. And count the patience of our Lord as salvation, just
> as our beloved brother Paul also wrote to you according to

the wisdom given him, as he does in all his letters when he speaks in them of these matters. There are some things in them that are hard to understand, which the ignorant and unstable twist to their own destruction, as they do the other Scriptures. You therefore, beloved, knowing this beforehand, take care that you are not carried away with the error of lawless people and lose your own stability. But grow in the grace and knowledge of our Lord and Savior Jesus Christ. To him be the glory both now and to the day of eternity. Amen. (2 Peter 3:14–18)

These verses in 2 Peter demonstrate exactly what it is to be weak and not exercise our faith. When we look at the current generations of self-proclaimed Christians in the US, we can easily see that many have not heeded these words. They have been carried away by the lawless; they have lost their stability. They have not exercised techniques in growing bold or chosen to pursue the truth. Instead, they have chosen the easy path and spouted a few words about Jesus without actually understanding in their hearts or seeking him out.

They have not lived a life inundated with prayer. They have not studied the Word of God. They have not submitted to the leadership of a trustworthy church and biblically astute pastor. Instead, they have allowed culture to weaken them, and they don't even see their destruction.

You need to get uncomfortable with new activities if you're going to avoid becoming one of these people. As you become comfortable, increase your actions to be uncomfortable again. This applies to so many areas of our lives, but the area of boldness is an important one.

What exactly are these techniques that help us grow bold? Yes, prayer and the study of Scripture are two critical components, so we will look at those, but we'll look at a few examples of others as well. We'll go further in depth in the following chapters.

Prayer

Prayer is a key aspect of our faith throughout the Bible, spanning the Old Testament and New from ancient Israel to every Sunday morning at church today. Many books, studies, and sermon series out there look at prayer from a deeper perspective and can help us distinguish every last element of growing in our prayer lives, but for now, let's consider it a valuable part of our life in knowing Christ. We learn prayer from him and use it to petition and seek him (the Lord's Prayer in Matthew 6:9–15). The verses throughout the Bible about prayer are seemingly endless, and we are constantly encouraged to pray for the following: what we need, our enemies, forgiveness, protection, and others. Essentially, we should go to God through Jesus with anything we wish to pray about.

The Bible warns us against abusing prayer or using it out of pride, but we are encouraged to grow in our faith through prayer. When we don't know what to pray, Romans 8:26 tells us, "Likewise the Spirit helps us in our weakness. For we do not know what to pray for as we ought, but the Spirit himself intercedes for us with groanings too deep for words."

Growing in boldness requires growing in prayer. Learn to pray boldly. Learn to pray, seek, ask, and knock for all the things on your heart. In humility, pray for them in light of the will of God but know he may not give you everything you pray for. Pray with the awareness of Romans 8:28, "And we know that for those who love God all things work together for good, for those who are called according to his purpose." So even if he doesn't give you the answer you want, he has given you the answer and the assurance that all things work for good.

From prayers of rejoicing, like Hannah's prayer in 1 Samuel to thank God for giving her a child, to prayers of grief, like Jesus prayed in the Garden of Gethsemane, we see prayer in nearly every context throughout the Bible. We see guidelines for prayer following the emergence of the Holy Spirit in Acts and how, if prayer is in another language, it requires interpretation to be considered legitimate, as opposed to random babbling meant to inspire or motivate.

With all this in mind, we have to decide how seriously we will take prayer. Will this be a gift we exercise and choose to grow? Will we allow prayer to become a bold, fearless part of our lives? Will we pray boldly, and will we allow prayer to make us bold?

Reading the Bible

Certainly, we can't know any what God's Word says about prayer if we aren't also reading it. For many believers in Christ, this is more difficult than prayer. After all, we can pray anywhere and anytime: consistently before meals, when we pass an accident on the highway, or when we're hoping to get out of a work meeting at work. And while these prayers may not be the deep intercession that leads to great boldness, they are still a way to exercise our faith.

But sitting down to read takes a little more effort. Maybe your Bible reading version of the quick "thank you for this day" prayer is to have a calendar on your desk with a daily Bible verse you read and think about. While it's nice to read even a verse a day, the Bible is a book divided into sixty-six books and taken in context.

Consider the quote, "What, you egg? [He stabs him]" If you saw that on someone's daily Shakespeare quote calendar, you would probably be extremely confused. Outside of the context of Act 4, Scene 2 of Macbeth, it makes very little sense. The same could be said about Deuteronomy 3:19, which says "(I know that you have much livestock)."

The Bible isn't meant to be stripped down, isolated verse by verse. It is meant to be read in its context. It is meant to be studied. And while yearly Bible reading plans can help some people, I'm not a fan of those that have you reading three separate books of the Bible each day rather than studying chapters in the context of the surrounding text.

Reading the Bible isn't a race, and it doesn't have to be completed in a year. It should be carefully, fruitfully read and understood. Yes, verses may pop out as extra important, and it is wonderful to memorize and learn them. But the Bible is the history of the world and of God becoming man to save man that man might glorify him. The Old Testament is not an out-of-date book of rules contradicted by the loving and good-vibes-only New Testament.

Rather, the Old Testament shows us a holy God who demands justice, and the New Testament reflects that justice through the saving work of Christ on the cross. The more we dig into what the Bible says and how it pieces together, the bolder we become in our understanding of the truth. We have a solid, firm foundation to stand on. Christ is the cornerstone, and we learn of him from the Bible (Psalm 118:22).

Bible study should absolutely be a part of our endurance and our growth in the faith. The more time you devote to the Scriptures, the more confident you will become in standing in obedience when it's difficult and in speaking the truth in love to those who do not know Jesus or who know a false version of him.

Church Attendance

The value of church attendance cannot be overstated. Especially since 2020, when everything went virtual, we have seen such a steep decline in how people feel about in-person church attendance.

Maybe it goes back to the issue of convenience, but many people so enjoyed watching church from home that they never bothered to return. Cell-phone tracking data shows that a mere 5 percent of Americans attend church weekly—as opposed to the 22 percent who claim to.[60] Perhaps those who claim to attend weekly are watching from home, or maybe they just want to make it sound like they go more often than they do.

Sure, you could argue that Grandma doesn't have an iPhone and geodata is imperfect. Besides, some people may leave their phones at home when they attend church. But overall, these statistics are still quite telling. It demonstrates just how significantly church attendance has dropped, given the fact that the majority of Americans do have phones with geodata, and most people keep their phones with them the majority of the time.

Many people think church membership is unimportant, and they don't mind being an anonymous member of a large church. Others don't feel that going to church is important at all because God can be worshipped anywhere.

People debate about what day to attend church and even the value of relevance of church attendance. But the Bible is clear that the church as a whole is a key piece of Christianity. Without the fellowship of believers, we will struggle to stand firm on our own.

You might try to justify not attending church because you're busy, work on Sundays, struggle with social anxiety, or you had a bad experience in the past. Regardless, I encourage you to look at what it really means to be a Christian in the context of the early church. It was never meant to be a place of gossip or stress. Humans are sinful

---

[60] Devin Pope, "Religious worship attendance in America: Evidence from Cellphone Data," 2024, BFI, https://bfi.uchicago.edu/insights/religious-worship-attendance-in-america-evidence-from-cellphone-data/.

and make church stressful at times, but the church is about Christ. And if we are in a gospel-preaching church and are there to grow in our faith, the rest will fall by the wayside.

Moving Forward

In the following chapters, we will go over these and other aspects of growing in our faith. As you look at what you can do to become bolder, I would encourage you to do the following:

1. Mark off what you do already.
2. Add one thing you can do, and do it consistently until you can do it for two weeks straight.
3. Add one more item, and continue doing that for two weeks until you get comfortable with it. Then add a third item. In this way, you will progressively growing in your faith to understand the truth. Don't get comfortable. Keep pushing.

When you start to falter, review the obstacles discussed above and ask yourself why you are struggling. Start working on it as you check off the items you want to complete.

Never lose sight of why you are striving for this lifestyle. Our own works don't save us but come out of the gratitude and mercy of the forgiveness we have in Christ. Your faith should not exhaust you as you exercise it. It should be a source of rest, peace, and strength, even as you keep pressing into God.

> Therefore do not throw away your confidence, which has a great reward. For you have need of endurance, so that when you have done the will of God you may receive what is promised. For,
>
> "Yet a little while,
>> and the coming one will come and will not delay;
> but my righteous one shall live by faith,
>> and if he shrinks back,
>> my soul has no pleasure in him."

But we are not of those who shrink back and are destroyed, but of those who have faith and preserve their souls. (Hebrew 10:35–39)

Your endurance, mentioned in this passage, isn't what saves you from your sin. Never get confused about the source of your salvation; only know that endurance is a gift to be pursued. So whether that endurance is related to prayer and reading the Bible or if it's about confession and learning the creeds of church history, continue growing. Continue seeking the techniques that will grow your faith and make you bold.

Remember that you are an ambassador for Christ in this world. As such, you have a responsibility to seek him, find your rest in him, and let that pour out into the lives of others.

For Reflection

1. How does prayer contribute to your growth in boldness or influenced your faith? Can you recall a time when boldness in prayer led to a significant change in your life? Consider a time when a bold, persistent prayer resulted in God's intervention and think about how you can deepen your boldness in prayer moving forward._

2. Spiritual growth is compared to physical exercise, where discomfort leads to growth. How does this analogy apply to your faith journey? What areas of your spiritual life currently feel uncomfortable, and how might this indicate growth? Think about areas of your faith that stretch you or make you uncomfortable. How might God be using these discomforts to grow you? Consider how you can embrace these challenges as opportunities for spiritual growth.

3. What could happen if you remain in your current level of faith without pushing yourself to grow? How does this connect with the warning in 2 Peter 3:17 about being carried away by the lawless? Reflect on the dangers of spiritual complacency. How can you actively seek spiritual growth to avoid stagnation, and how does this strengthen your ability to stand firm in your faith?

4. How do you engage with Scripture to grow in boldness for Christ? How does understanding the Bible as a whole—rather than isolated verses—shape your faith? Consider how regular engagement with the whole counsel of God's Word strengthens your boldness and leads to a deeper trust and confidence in your faith.

5. What might happen if you neglect regular church attendance? How can you encourage others to prioritize gathering with the body of Christ? Think about the impact regular church attendance has on your spiritual growth and boldness. How can you encourage others to remain committed to the body of Christ, especially during challenging times?

CHAPTER FIFTEEN

Repent

Repentance is a critical part of the journey to becoming and growing as a Christian, a fruit of salvation in lives of believers. When John the Baptist, Peter, Paul, and Jesus taught, they spoke of repentance as a necessary component of true salvation. In fact, all four of them spoke of repentance in the very first sermon they preached. This was clearly important to them; therefore, it must be important to us.

Repentance doesn't mean saying "I am sorry" or "My bad." Repentance involves two acts. First, it requires confessing that the sin is wrong, and from there, we must make changes to turn from that sin. The confessing part seems pretty easy. After all, small children can say, "I'm sorry." However, they might follow that up with, "It was just an accident."

We do the same thing. We may confess our sins, but then we excuse the sin.

- "It's not my fault."
- "They did it first."
- "Everybody does it."

Confession with an excuse is not even close to repentance. The excuse is saying, "My behavior is justified for this reason." If your behavior is excused, then you cannot acknowledge it as wrong at the same time. These two perspectives are mutually exclusive.

But as hard as it is to confess without an excuse, turning it around can be extremely difficult. This part can take a long time, depending on how deep the sin is entrenched in your life. But what effort are you making to do so?

The Bible tells us what to do when we feel godly grief and how that leads to repentance.

> As it is, I rejoice, not because you were grieved, but because you were grieved into repenting. For you felt a godly grief, so that you suffered no loss through us.
>
> For godly grief produces a repentance that leads to salvation without regret, whereas worldly grief produces death. For see what earnestness this godly grief has produced in you, but also what eagerness to clear yourselves, what indignation, what fear, what longing, what zeal, what punishment! At every point you have proved yourselves innocent in the matter. (2 Corinthians 7:9–11)

When we first become Christians, we talk about how we have been justified. Through the work of Christ on the cross, we have obtained the gift of salvation. But the next step is our sanctification so that we can grow to be more like Jesus in terms of obedience to his law, resulting from his grace. Through sanctification, we stop pursuing sin and wickedness and begin to live in a manner worthy of the truth.

Repentance is part of that sanctification. When we repent, we truly seek forgiveness and turn away from those sinful habits, letting them go and not living under the yoke of slavery to our flesh any longer.

What does this look like in your life? It really depends. For some, repentance may mean asking forgiveness for a porn addiction, then determining to be held accountable. Someone struggling with this issue may talk to a close friend and sign up for accountability software that sends reports if they end up on a site they shouldn't be on. Then, day by day, they exercise self-control and seek the strength of Jesus to reject and deny those urges.

The same could be said for alcohol, lying, manipulation,

laziness, gluttony, or any other sin we find ourselves falling into. It can also apply to a lack of boldness and repenting for our former unwillingness to step out in faith and follow the urging in our hearts to boldly proclaim our faith and live in obedience to God and his Word. We have to look at and acknowledge the consequences of failing to be bold and make a decision as to how we should proceed.

Repentance is not remorse and regret. Judas was filled with remorse—and he ultimately killed himself. If he had repented, he would have been forgiven. But rather than repent, he simply felt remorse and understood the wickedness of his betrayal. Remorse means you feel bad for the harm you did to others. Just as Judas felt remorse for doing something so cruel as handing Jesus over to the enemy, our remorse leads us to that sick feeling in the pit of our stomach telling us how deeply vile our actions truly are.

Regret, on the other hand, is focused on missed opportunities or a personal loss. It's wishing we could go back and do something differently. It is regret that leads us to the aching desire to go back and have a do over of a circumstance so we get different results. We may regret a bad bet on the stock market or missing the chance to begin a relationship with someone before they met someone else.

We can't allow ourselves to confuse remorse and regret with the idea of repentance. While the feelings of remorse and regret can lead to action, repentance is an action in itself. It is the turning around. And while it can come about as a result of the other two, it involves a firm decision to move beyond the issue.

I always think back to a few specific circumstances in my own life where my regret for a missed opportunity led me to make a different choice.

In the first circumstance, I had gone to Vegas for a convention. Early in the morning, I woke up and was lying there, not wanting to get out of bed just yet. I felt the Holy Spirit telling me to get up and go for a walk, but I decided to rest just a bit longer. I was tired and really didn't feel like it. (When we're tired, it's extremely easy to ignore the nagging of the Holy Spirit and write it off as sleep deprivation.)

But that nagging sensation continued all morning and was still there when I heard a loud banging on my door. I went to the door to see who it was, but no one was in the hall. Whoever it may have been—a drunk person running down the hall or a maid trying to rush through her early morning duties—I'll never know. What I did know was that I'd been ignoring the sense I needed to get up and go for a walk. By this time, I got the point and myself together to go for a walk.

The night before, a rapper had performed in town, which meant general chaos abounded. I could smell pot everywhere when I got to the hotel, so I wasn't entirely surprised that in the early hours, a number of people were still wandering the streets dressed as if they had not gone to bed.

As I was leaving the hotel, some scantily dressed women were outside. They looked like they'd been to the concert and were heading home. At one point, they were at the crosswalk, the same one I was going to. They waited for the light to change, and I hung back about twenty feet, also waiting. I didn't want to get too close and creep them out, so I kept my distance and paid attention to the light without staring in their direction.

But as I busily distracted myself, one of the young women came over to me and asked for the time. I answered as briefly as possible. She then asked why I was in town, and I tried my best to keep my answer short so I wouldn't have to engage in conversation. The young woman asked what I was doing that morning and then offered to go back to my room with me to "have some fun."

I panicked. Realizing I was speaking with a prostitute, I simply said I needed to call my wife. The young ladies walked off, and I went in the other direction and called my wife, still quite shaken by the encounter.

A lot of Christians might pat me on the back for my response. Didn't I act just like Joseph, fleeing from Potiphar's wife? (Genesis 39) Surely I had done the right thing by running off to call my wife instead of furthering any conversation with a loose and wayward woman.

But I had missed something very pivotal. I'd had an opportunity to talk to these young women about Jesus. This girl had offered me an open door to discuss the truth, to explain why I couldn't engage in any activities she suggested. She had come to me and begun the conversation, and I had a chance, then and there, to tell her about God, to share my faith in Christ, to explain the hope of God's mercy.

Maybe this story and this moment weren't about me fleeing the temptation of sin. Maybe it was about her and her need to hear the truth. And maybe, when I didn't respond with the truth, God sent someone else her way. I'll never know. What I do know is I wasn't prepared when I should have been. I was trying to do the right thing, and I forgot to do the gospel thing.

I later prayed and repented, making a decision not to miss those types of opportunities again. When people approach me, I'm always looking for opportunities to share Jesus, regardless of the circumstance.

Of course, that doesn't mean I'm perfect. And while I truly wish I could say that was the last time I missed a chance to share the gospel with a hooker in Vegas, I made a similar mistake on one other occasion but for different reasons.

One way I try to serve my wife is by getting her coffee in the mornings if I'm at home and I'm up before her. When we are out of town, if the hotel room doesn't have coffee, I'll go down to the breakfast area and get some for her, then take it back to our room.

On a different trip to Vegas, I took my wife to a Garth Brooks concert, which was much different from the one I'd encountered in the previous story. So one morning, I went down to get her coffee from the hotel's breakfast area.

Right outside the elevator was a woman whom I assumed to be a concierge. It took a while to realize that she, too, was a hooker, but she made a similar offer to go to my room. At that point, I had to make another choice. I could go and sit with a prostitute in the breakfast area, having coffee with her and telling her about the gospel, or I could refuse the offer and get some coffee to take back up to my wife—who would not have been thrilled to come downstairs to find me sitting with another woman.

This wasn't necessarily an issue of not being prepared, but it does go back to the issue of convenience. It would have been extremely inconvenient to spend time with this woman right then. My wife wouldn't have appreciated it, and she would have been inconvenienced because she didn't know where I was and didn't have her coffee. The timing just wasn't right.

Again, maybe I justified myself in that moment by saying that I was considering my wife above this woman. After all, God gave me a duty to protect and provide for my wife, so she should have been my first priority. But whether I liked it or not, I also had to face the fact that I was not bold in a situation where boldness would have been honoring to God.

I really didn't feel bad, but I realized the importance of not missing opportunities to speak with those who are lost and telling them about Jesus. Repentance leads us to determining that we will always, no matter the cost, speak up for truth and step out in boldness, even if it's inconvenient and even if we are caught off guard.

The Westminster Shorter Catechism #87 gives us this question and answer about repentance:

Q: What is repentance unto life?[61]

A: Repentance unto life is a saving grace, whereby a sinner, out of a true sense of his sin, and apprehension of the mercy of God in Christ, does, with grief and hatred of his sin, turn from it unto God, with full purpose of, and endeavor after, new obedience.

If this is how we define repentance, why is repentance bold?

Repentance is hard. It's not easy to walk away from the flesh. The Bible is clear about how challenging it is to let go of our sin, but it also shows us the importance of doing just that. So to repent and turn away from our sin and our mistakes is a bold move.

Without repentance, we cannot move past our old life and enter into the next life where we are honoring God through obedience. Moreover, you cannot be bold if you won't repent for the sins you are aware of. That means you are still living in bondage to the will of the flesh (Romans 6:16).

You can be held back (fail to be bold) by focusing on what a sinner you are and what sins you are hiding from the world. After all, our shame keeps us down. If we can't seem to turn away from it, we feel like hypocrites. How can a hypocrite witness to others about the grace and mercy of Jesus? How can a hypocrite call others to repent if we can't do it ourselves?

We truly can't expect to be change-makers in our own strength,

---

[61] "Shorter Catechism," The Orthodox Presbyterian Church, accessed May 17, 2025, https://opc.org/sc.html.

so we need to grow in Christ, and a part of that is this repentance, which is a biblical cause for celebration.

> So he told them this parable: "What man of you, having a hundred sheep, if he has lost one of them, does not leave the ninety-nine in the open country, and go after the one that is lost, until he finds it? And when he has found it, he lays it on his shoulders, rejoicing. And when he comes home, he calls together his friends and his neighbors, saying to them, 'Rejoice with me, for I have found my sheep that was lost.' Just so, I tell you, there will be more joy in heaven over one sinner who repents than over ninety-nine righteous persons who need no repentance." (Luke 15:3–7)

Think of each obstacle in the previous chapters. By now, you know which ones resonate the most with you, whether it's an issue of confidence, comfort, or convenience—or something else altogether. If these are preventing you from being bold, then repentance is the only way past this. You have to seek God and ask him to help you get over this issue that's holding you back.

We need to humble ourselves when we repent. This is critical for many reasons, including the reality that the only way to cast our anxieties on Jesus is by being humble. Humbling ourselves allows us to open doors without pride jumping in on potential losses.

Most of our issues arise because we aren't putting our faith in Jesus. We are afraid of something, and we don't want to let go of that fear. Yes, this can go back to the idea of control, but with any of the obstacles, we are required to lean on him for strength. The source of your struggle might not simply be convenience but anxiety. For example, if God asks for your five minutes now, you won't have that five minutes later to finish your work deadlines. If you struggle with this, it's time to repent.

Forgiveness as Repentance

It's important to forgive, not because you are a nice person but because you are not a nice person. Forgiveness is an act of repentance. We must forgive others so that we don't hold anger in our hearts. Once we forgive, we can turn around and go in the other direction. We are no longer poisoning our own souls with anger or pain, but we are giving way to freedom.

Forgiveness is also an act of boldness because no one does it. You have to be able to forgive others. When people see you act so boldly, it should always be the result of how Jesus told us to live in a world that encourages disunity, fighting, insults, bullying, etc.

We are called to live differently. You are acting against the world, which is always seen as a bold act. Whenever you hear stories of parents who forgive their child's killers, a frequent response is, "Well, they are better people than me." We recognize that nearly everyone struggles to forgive such a heinous crime, and we recognize it is a better trait—even when we know we cannot do it.

Forgiveness is always conditional. The Bible tells you to forgive so that you can be forgiven. When you forgive others, it frees you from the bondage of your own bitterness. You avoid letting hurt, anger, and pain take root in you. Those things can poison your hearts. But if you reach for forgiveness, showing mercy and grace to others as it has been extended to you, you are free to receive even more of the grace and mercy of God.

Repentance is a gift. This truly special, humbling mercy is that we get to seek God's forgiveness and can lean on his strength to let go of our sinfulness. And when the world tries to remind us of our hypocrisies and failures, we lean further into the Word of God and remember what he had to say about the matter.

> After this he went out and saw a tax collector named Levi, sitting at the tax booth. And he said to him, "Follow me." And leaving everything, he rose and followed him.
>
> And Levi made him a great feast in his house, and there was a large company of tax collectors and others reclining at table with them. And the Pharisees and their scribes grumbled at his disciples, saying, "Why do you eat and drink with tax collectors and sinners?" And Jesus answered them, "Those who are well have no need of a physician, but those who are sick. I have not come to call the righteous but sinners to repentance."
>
> And they said to him, "The disciples of John fast often and offer prayers, and so do the disciples of the Pharisees, but yours eat and drink." And Jesus said to them, "Can you make wedding guests fast while the bridegroom is with them? The days will come when the bridegroom is taken

away from them, and then they will fast in those days." He also told them a parable: "No one tears a piece from a new garment and puts it on an old garment. If he does, he will tear the new, and the piece from the new will not match the old. And no one puts new wine into old wineskins. If he does, the new wine will burst the skins and it will be spilled, and the skins will be destroyed. But new wine must be put into fresh wineskins. And no one after drinking old wine desires new, for he says, 'The old is good.'" (Luke 5:27–39)

For Reflection

1. What is the difference between remorse, regret, and repentance, and how can you distinguish between them in your own life? Reflect on the moments when you've felt remorse or regret. How can you ensure that you are moving toward true repentance, which involves a change of heart and action, rather than just feeling sorry?

2. Why is repentance more than just saying "I'm sorry"? Think about a time when you truly repented for something in your life and experienced change. Reflect on how repentance requires both a change of heart and a change in action.

3. In 2 Corinthians 7:9–11, Paul contrasts godly grief with worldly grief. Reflect on the difference between godly grief and worldly grief in your own life. How does godly grief lead to true repentance, and how might worldly grief prevent this process? How does true repentance, driven by godly grief, lead to transformation in your faith?

4. Repentance is described as a "bold move." In what ways does true repentance require courage or boldness in your life? Consider how repentance demands humility and boldness. Reflect on the courage required to acknowledge sin and take steps toward change, especially when it involves personal sacrifice.

5. How does fear and anxiety hold us back from being bold in our repentance? What steps can we take to overcome these obstacles? How can you push past negative emotions and rely on God's grace to boldly turn from sin and seek his forgiveness?

6. How does humility open the door for true repentance and transformation? How does pride interfere with this process?

7. Repentance involves turning away from sin and moving toward obedience. Consider areas where you need to turn away from sin and embrace greater obedience to God. What specific areas of your life do you need to turn away from and be obedient to God?

Reflect on how this process of turning from sin can deepen your relationship with Him.

8. In Luke 15, the parable of the lost sheep reminds us that heaven rejoices over one sinner who repents. How does this parable shape your understanding of repentance? Reflect on times when you feel lost and distant from God. Were you holding on to sin while God wanted you to return?

CHAPTER SIXTEEN

Read the Bible

In chapter 14, we looked briefly at three techniques for boldness. Now, we can dive in deeper and consider just how valuable it is to exercise these techniques and more. Because the Bible is such an important foundation of our faith, we'll begin there. After all, this book shows us the importance of all the other ways to grow in our faith and tells us the true character of whom we serve.

Reading the Bible is an act of boldness. It is hard to be bold when we are not comfortable with our level of knowledge, but it is also hard to be bold when we do not have a daily relationship with God. If our only knowledge of the Bible is what we hear preached at church on Sundays, we won't even know if our pastor is preaching accurately or in context. Instead, the Bible needs to be a part of our daily lives and routines so we might grow in understanding and real faith. The more you read the Bible, the more God's Word enters your heart and the more you believe it. From there, you won't have to worry so much about the external pressures.

During one important moment, I was reminded of the value of knowing Scripture in our hearts. I was at court with a guy who works for me. He trains prep cooks and shares the gospel with them, but his testimony goes back to when he first became a Christian while in jail. He started with our company as a prep cook but has since moved in a different direction and is quite prominent in our restaurants.

At this time, he was changing probation officers, moving from a more restrictive tier to a less restrictive tier. There was some confusion over where he was supposed to go, and ultimately, he went to the wrong place and had to go to court because it looked like he missed his probation meeting.

I went with him on the court date to support him, knowing it had all just been a misunderstanding. If the worst-case scenario came to pass and he was in trouble, I represent him and ask for a continuance until a new attorney could be appointed.

There I was, sitting with my Bible, and I looked up at a verse etched into the side of the courthouse. Then, the court clerk came in and handed papers to those who were there to see the judge. They had to fill the papers out for the proceeding. It was clear I didn't necessarily fit in. As he came by, the clerk glared at me. "Why are you here?" I explained the situation, but the clerk just looked away. But then he looked down at the Bible. "Don't open that book in here."

I took a deep breath so that I didn't respond to his rudeness in a way that was out of character for a Christian. I was there to support my employee and didn't want to make matters complicated or get us into any further trouble. I could have easily cast aside boldness and let belligerence run my mouth. After all, who was this clerk to tell me I couldn't open my Bible? It seemed like a potential lawsuit for religious freedom.

But I didn't respond. My employee sat calmly beside me. "We don't have to open the book. The Word is in our hearts."

I admit to being more indignant and quick-tempered than my employee, but he was absolutely right. The Bible is a book of value and importance, but if it lives in our hearts, no one can take it away from us. It is not only written on paper, but it is given by God for our benefit. "All Scripture is breathed out by God and profitable for teaching, for reproof, for correction, and for training in righteousness, that the man of God may be complete, equipped for every good work" (2 Timothy 3:16–17).

Many people in this world don't want us to read the Bible, but we don't have to be limited by their rules or commands. If we read it regularly, we can roll with what they say if they try to stop us. We can live with what we know in our hearts.[62]

When you read the Bible, you're spending time with God. He will help you discern what he says and means. Some will come at it from an academic mindset and may try to twist or reinterpret the Word of God in false ways meant to trip us up. Even in the Bible, this happened. But when we live with the daily, consistent pursuit of God's Word and when we understand the context, we can avoid such traps.

Jesus set this example for us. While we will never have the understanding and wisdom that he has, we can still be diligent to stand firm in the truth and pursue a better knowledge of the Bible than those who are twisting it.

> The same day Sadducees came to him, who say that there is no resurrection, and they asked him a question, saying, "Teacher, Moses said, 'If a man dies having no children, his brother must marry the widow and raise up offspring for his brother.' Now there were seven brothers among us. The first married and died, and having no offspring left his wife to his brother. So too the second and third, down to the seventh. After them all, the woman died. In the resurrection, therefore, of the seven, whose wife will she be? For they all had her."
>
> But Jesus answered them, "You are wrong, because you know neither the Scriptures nor the power of God. For in the resurrection they neither marry nor are given in marriage, but are like angels in heaven. And as for the resurrection of the dead, have you not read what was said to you by God: 'I am the God of Abraham, and the God of Isaac, and the God of Jacob?' He is not God of the dead, but of the living." And when the crowd heard it, they were astonished at his teaching. (Matthew 22:23–33)

As previously mentioned, I am not opposed to a yearly reading

---

[62] The post-apocalyptic film *The Book of Eli* demonstrates the value of knowing Scripture in our hearts, particularly during dark times when the world wants to abolish or even twist the truth to fit their own desire for power. (Note: Be aware that this movie has a significant amount of violence.) While this is a surprising message from a Hollywood production, it's an important reminder of why daily, consistent reading and studying the Word matters.

plan, but it seems ineffective for most people. We might start off well, but when we miss a few days at some point and get discouraged, feeling like it would take a lot of energy to catch up, human nature tells us to just quit.

Instead, if you read the Bible systematically in order for fifteen minutes a day, you will find some days, you read a lot and, other days, you will focus and obsess over one verse. Either way, you're working your way through the Bible and devoting a portion of your day to diving into the Word instead of marking day 264 off your New Year's resolution checklist to read the Bible in a year.

It's actually quite exciting to spend that fifteen minutes reading every day. Sometimes what I read confuses me, and I need to research what the verse is saying. Other times, I get inspired, and I want to meditate on what I've just read. Some days, fifteen minutes pass, and I keep going. Other days, I think fifteen minutes is almost up and see that six minutes have passed. I read the Bible in spite of how I feel.

It's helpful to create systems for reading the Bible that work with your schedule. I get up early in the morning, so I read my Bible before I do anything else. This is just what works for me. Others, I know, read before bed. Some read on their lunch break. Often, young families will do a family reading after dinner to get their children involved and may change the routine as the children get older.

What works with your schedule? What works with your life? You decide what will be the most effective, but do not imitate other people just because you think that's how it's supposed to work. How others spend their time may not be the best way for you to spend yours.

When you read more, your desire to read more and spend more time with him will then increase. This process often goes from discipline to desire to delight. You won't want to read every day, and sometimes you will just struggle. These are the hardest yet the most important days. Engage the muscles of discipline. Do the workout. Eventually, it gets easier and becomes a habit you look forward to. And when the off days do occasionally occur, you will be so in the habit that your day will feel too strange to go without it.

Once you have totally engaged in a lifestyle that values daily reading, you naturally tell people what you read about. They also start to ask when they see how it applies in your life. The more you read, the more you can discuss the impact of your Bible reading and study.

A few days prior to writing this section, I was reading 2 Peter. As it happened, I later interviewed a false prophet on my podcast. He was trying to sell gold and silver as a supposed biblical mandate based on his readings of Daniel and Revelation.

You may be surprised how often that happens once you really dive into your reading of the Word. At first, weird skin conditions in Leviticus may seem dull and, frankly, quite gross. But whether you then have a literal context where that Scripture becomes a helpful medical text or if it suddenly wakes you up to just how deep the law of God goes and how inherently desperate we are for a Savior who can rescue us from the isolating rules of purification, you start to see those verses in a new light.

Job's friends seem to drone on and on, and you just want to skip what they're saying, but on the dark days when you feel alone or misunderstood in your trials, Job's story becomes a source of great comfort. Then, the rebuke against his friends will bring you some vindication that helps you forgive those in your life who act like Job's friends instead of growing bitter and self-pitying.

Paul's admonitions against some of the churches in the New Testament may seem dull or mean-spirited until you see how very little human failures have changed in the church as a whole in the centuries since. The context of the Bible brings light to our modern understanding and gives us a better realization of what's really happening. Otherwise, we are just as bad as the scholars of Jesus's day.

> And the Father who sent me has himself borne witness about me. His voice you have never heard, his form you have never seen, and you do not have his word abiding in you, for you do not believe the one whom he has sent. You search the Scriptures because you think that in them you have eternal life; and it is they that bear witness about me, yet you refuse to come to me that you may have life. (John 5:37–40)

Next, as your reading becomes a habit, keep a Bible out where people can see it. Mine is usually on my desk and always in my backpack. We buy Gideon New Testament Bibles, and I place them in our restaurants for customers to take if they want to. In general, we make every effort for the Bible to be seen and available. It's a way of normalizing the presence of Scripture while also opening doors for conversations so that others can begin a daily relationship with Christ.

I'm often surprised by how frequently people inquire if I am a minister, pastor, or preacher when they see me carrying my Bible. Just recently, while walking to a park, I was approached by someone involved in a recovery program who assumed my role based on the presence of my Bible.

Similarly, when my wife and I travel, I often retreat from my hotel room to a lobby or somewhere to read, so as not to disturb her, and this practice often prompts questions about my profession. Even in hospitals, where one might expect spiritual guidance and support, the sight of my Bible leads people to ask about my ministerial role.

This recurring curiosity raises an interesting question: Why do people equate the presence of a Bible with being a minister? The assumption seems to be that only clergy can offer prayer and spiritual support. Yet we must remember that prayer and communication with God are not limited to ordained ministers; they are accessible to all believers through the Holy Spirit, regardless of one's occupation.

What concerns me is that when I am not carrying my Bible, no one assumes I am a minister or asks for prayer. This discrepancy highlights a broader issue: the rarity of seeing Bibles in public spaces has led to the misconception that carrying one signifies a professional role rather than a personal practice. We seem to have become so accustomed to seeing the Bible as a symbol of clergy that its presence is more closely associated with professional ministry than with personal faith.

As such, it is an act of boldness to be public with our reading of Scripture, not out of pride or a holier-than-thou attitude like we often see with the Pharisees in the New Testament but as a means of again normalizing the presence of God's Word. While personal Bible reading at home is important, you can also enjoy reading a passage at your local coffee shop or a park.

If it became normal for people in our culture to see us taking our reading seriously in public, they would probably make less assumptions about people walking around with their Bibles. It's a simple, small means of influencing culture.

Eric Metaxas once came to my restaurant, and he preached at our church, saying that the presence of small pocket New Testaments at the front of the restaurant for people to take was a step of boldness. This sort of boldness doesn't cost us much financially or in terms of convenience and conflict, which can make a larger impact. Will some people not like it and possibly speak out? Sure. But does that matter in the larger view of things?

Not even a little bit.

What's most important is that you apply what you read to others around you. For teamwork issues, talk about Nehemiah and how this book relates to teamwork. After all, there is nothing new under the sun (Ecclesiastes 1:9). We can find and apply Scripture for nearly every situation we experience.

In our business, I've had opportunities to improve our strategies, thanks to what I've read in the Bible. From COVID to the time of this writing and probably beyond, for instance, the restaurant industry struggled significantly. We faced massive supply chain issues, making it nearly impossible to run a business. We could hardly get any product at all, causing huge problems for us and for our customers.

I had recently read Genesis 41, when Joseph tells Pharaoh about the seven years of plenty followed by seven years of famine. We found ourselves in the midst of a product famine. We couldn't get trash bags, straws, cups for our soup—which is one of our best sellers. Sometimes we were down to a mere sixty items, which certainly wasn't enough to keep a restaurant running for more than a day at a time.

With that in mind, I instituted our Genesis 41 plan. We struggled through that season, but as products became available once more, we determined we would never be in that situation again. We wouldn't be in competition with other restaurants in the midst of depleted supplies. Instead, we would stock our store houses.

I began ordering a four-week supply of every nonperishable item as stock began to improve. Then, if the suppliers did happen to run out, we could distribute those items to our restaurants without missing a beat. Ironically, a four-week supply of every nonperishable item filled seven storage units, which became our seven storage units of plenty.

Reading God's Word has allowed us to get through seasons like this and will prevent us from struggling in future circumstances when we may face similar situations. If we already have those items on hand, we won't find ourselves in a 2020 toilet paper situation. Instead, we are using the wisdom of Scripture to prepare.

When reading the Bible systematically, God so often answers our prayers through it. Helter-skelter reading isn't as effective. Instead, we have the opportunity to use the wisdom of the Word to take advantage of opportunities we may not have otherwise seen. Stockpiling to beat supply chain disruptions or inflation may not be the answer to the prayer you're currently praying, but another topic in the Bible might apply to you.

Meticulous and consistent study of the Bible doesn't have to be painful or boring or overwhelming. It's a gift. We have an amazing opportunity, given by God, to hear him speak to us that allows us to grow in our understanding while also finding the answers to the aches and pains of daily life. We can come to God as the psalmist did, asking for understanding and wisdom.

> Let my cry come before you, O Lord;
>> give me understanding according to your word!
> Let my plea come before you;
>> deliver me according to your word.
> My lips will pour forth praise,
>> for you teach me your statutes.
> My tongue will sing of your word,
>> for all your commandments are right.
> Let your hand be ready to help me,
>> for I have chosen your precepts.
> I long for your salvation, O Lord,
>> and your law is my delight.
> Let my soul live and praise you,
>> and let your rules help me.
> I have gone astray like a lost sheep; seek your servant,
>> for I do not forget your commandments.
> (Psalm 119:169–176)

Through the reading of the Bible and teaching it to others—whether our children, our employees, or even a hooker in Vegas—we can live a life of strength and boldness. We have the confidence and assurance that we are standing in the truth.

For Reflection

1. Reflect on the author's assertion that reading the Bible is an act of boldness. How does reading the Bible help you build a stronger relationship with God? How does daily engagement with His Word shape your understanding of Him and increase your boldness in faith?

2. The author discusses the importance of knowing Scripture for both personal growth and discernment. In your life, how do you balance head knowledge of Scripture with a heart relationship with God? How can you deepen your connection with God through Scripture while avoiding just accumulating information?

3. The author shares a story about carrying a Bible in public and how it invites curiosity and questions. How might your public display of reading or carrying a Bible invite conversations or opportunities to share your faith? How can you create space for conversations about faith by openly engaging with the Bible in public places?

4. In the courtroom scenario, the clerk orders the author not to open the Bible. Reflect on the employee's response: "The Word is in our hearts." How does this response model boldness and trust in God's Word, even when external obstacles arise?

5. The author suggests that carrying a Bible in public is an act of boldness. What does it mean to be bold in your faith in public spaces? What are the challenges and benefits of doing so? Think about what it means to live out your faith openly in public. What are the risks and rewards of being bold in expressing your beliefs, especially in environments that may not support Christianity?

6. The author writes about how their Bible reading informs their actions and character. Can you recall a specific situation where a passage from the Bible influenced the way you responded to a challenge or person? How can your consistent engagement with the Bible continue to influence your character and behavior?

7. Think about the ways your daily reading of Scripture can

impact those around you. How can you intentionally apply biblical truths in your interactions, making a positive impact in your family, workplace, or community?

8. The author acknowledges that it will not be easy to engage with Scripture every day. Consider the obstacles you face in maintaining a consistent Bible reading habit. What specific steps can you take to overcome distractions and cultivate a deeper commitment to engaging with God's Word?

9. In what ways can your commitment to reading the Bible create opportunities to engage others in spiritual conversations, particularly those who might not yet know Christ? Think about how your practice of reading Scripture can create open doors to share your faith. How might your actions and conversations encourage others to explore or question their beliefs?

10. How can you encourage others around you to take up the daily habit of reading the Bible without making it feel like a checklist or obligation? Reflect on how you can inspire others to develop a love for Scripture.

11. Consider the cultural challenges in publicly displaying the Bible. How can you help shift the narrative by confidently and respectfully normalizing Scripture in everyday conversations and spaces?

CHAPTER SEVENTEEN

Pray

Prayer (I)

Prayer the church's banquet, angel's age,
God's breath in man returning to his birth,
The soul in paraphrase, heart in pilgrimage,
The Christian plummet sounding heav'n and earth
Engine against th' Almighty, sinner's tow'r,
Reversed thunder, Christ-side-piercing spear,
The six-days world transposing in an hour,
A kind of tune, which all things hear and fear;
Softness, and peace, and joy, and love, and bliss,
Exalted manna, gladness of the best,
Heaven in ordinary, man well drest,
The milky way, the bird of Paradise,
Church-bells beyond the stars heard, the soul's blood,
The land of spices; something understood.[63]

The next step to boldness is prayer. This probably seems like an

---

[63] George Herbert, "Selected Poem – 'Prayer (I)'" George Herbert, accessed May 17, 2025, https://www.georgeherbert.org.uk/archives/selected_work_27.html.

activity that can be done all the time, but there is a difference between praying at home as you drift to sleep and praying boldly. As we talked about previously, we often think prayer is easier than reading the Bible since it can be done anywhere, any time, but is that really how we should pray? Does prayer mean we conveniently spout a few words here and there, or does it mean interceding before the throne of God above? Should it be done whenever it's easy, or should it be a matter of reverence and humility?

The answer should be clear. Pray at any and all times, no matter what. But pray with fervent respect and with true faith and trust. Our prayers should always be the result of hearts that lean into the truth of God's Word, thanking him for his mercy and submitting to his will. We can't take the gift of prayer and the ability to connect with God anytime for granted. This is one of the most critical components of our walk with God.

You might struggle to pray out loud in front of friends or coworkers, especially when you first start. I have dealt with this myself on more than one occasion. You start to pray, and then Satan enters your mind and starts giving you all the reasons in the world why you should not pray. Then, you fail afterward because time lapses, and now it is even more awkward. You may trip over your tongue and then lose confidence the next time you have a chance to pray out loud.

Or you may just be uncertain from the beginning and not sure how to get over your discomfort. The fact is, learning to pray isn't as simple as it sounds when we don't give ourselves a chance to grow. We have to submit to the importance of prayer and of always turning to God.

Even at Christian schools, groups of teenagers might be too scared to pray out loud when asked to do so. However, this is not limited to young people. Christians at Bible studies are sometimes afraid to pray as well.

People seem to be scared to pray out loud because they are worried about what others might think of their prayer and, by extension, them personally. Instead, they need to focus on the wonder and marvel of talking to the God of the universe who created them. Furthermore, people do not seem to pray out loud consistently at home. When we pray out loud at home, we have the opportunity to get used to the sound of our own voice. We can practice prayer in a disciplined, God-fearing manner. With that in mind, practice helps remove the doubts and worries we otherwise have as far as how others may respond.

It doesn't matter if your pastor has eight Ivy League degrees and prays in such a way that the congregation needs an *Oxford Dictionary* to follow along. The rest of the people in your church are not going to look down on you for not always having the right words to pray. And if they do, that's certainly a problem with their own hearts.

The more we pray and connect with God In our own homes, the easier it becomes to do so outside the home. We grow in comfort and understanding of how to pray, and we certainly increase our *longing* to pray.

The Lord's Prayer gives us a simple blueprint for prayer that we can follow, and sometimes, it may be worthwhile to pray that each day as we learn to grow in our prayer lives. But the beauty of walking with God is that we can take all petitions to him and seek his guidance in all things.

Pray over your calendar for the day. Invite God into the meetings you will have. Pray over family members who may be struggling or whom you desire to know God better. Pray over your children for that day and the years to follow. Pray over your spouse that their life will be full of the wonder of God. Pray over your house payment or whatever worries may be weighing on your shoulders.

There is nothing too small to pray about.

> But will God indeed dwell on the earth? Behold, heaven and the highest heaven cannot contain you; how much less this house that I have built! Yet have regard to the prayer of your servant and to his plea, O Lord my God, listening to the cry and to the prayer that your servant prays before you this day, that your eyes may be open night and day toward this house, the place of which you have said, "My name shall be there," that you may listen to the prayer that your servant offers toward this place. (1 Kings 8:27–29)

God hears the cries of our hearts, and the last thing we need to do is try to make them pretty or worth his while. A father is thrilled to hear from his child, and God certainly honors our true, heartfelt prayers with his listening ear.

The practice of prayer helps us be bold and encourages us to trust him when it's difficult and when our circumstances are less than ideal. Putting our faith in Christ alone is a tenet of Christianity and there's no better way to place our faith in him than to cast all our burdens on him in prayer?

One of the most significant aspects of prayer is that it does not have to be eloquent. The beauty of prayer lies in its authenticity. Simple heartfelt prayers are just as powerful as those that are more structured and formal. This accessibility ensures that anyone, regardless of their verbal skills, can engage in meaningful prayer.

> Come and hear, all you who fear God,
> and I will tell what he has done for my soul.
> I cried to him with my mouth,
> and high praise was on my tongue.
> If I had cherished iniquity in my heart,
> the Lord would not have listened.
> But truly God has listened;
> he has attended to the voice of my prayer.
> Blessed be God,
> because he has not rejected my prayer
> or removed his steadfast love from me!
> (Psalm 66:16–20)

This psalm isn't about perfectly worded prayers being answered but the humblest, most genuine and honest prayers. And while we can get to the matter of answered versus unanswered prayers, we must not forget that regardless of your prayer's outcomes, God still hears you.

One of the simplest prayers in the Bible is when Mary prays, "There is no wine." She looked at God and told him the problem. Then she trusted, by faith, afterward when she told the servant, "Do whatever he says." She did not know what he would do, but she trusted in the outcome. She knew it was in his hands.

Some brush prayer aside for this very reason. They say it's pointless to pray if God is sovereign anyway and will do his will regardless of our petitions and requests. Others abuse the idea of prayer in the opposite way, believing prayers prayed in faith will always be answered and that God's will is swayed by our belief we will get what we want. Both of these perspectives are dangerous and inaccurate.

To cast aside the very idea of prayer because of God's sovereign will is to disobey Scripture and to miss out on opportunities to draw near to God. Prayer is an act that builds faith. It doesn't merely benefit us because God may give us the answer we want through our prayer. It benefits us because it trains our hearts to lean on him and to learn to trust him through the good and the bad. On the other hand, believing that God is a genie who will grant our wishes if only we believe enough is powerfully disrespectful. It turns God into a creature of our own making and in our own image. It flaunts our man-centered wishes above the grace and mercy given to us by a righteous Savior. This perspective treats our faith as more powerful than God himself.

We must always consider prayer in light of what it really means and why we place our hope in his hands. To do anything less is to have a false view of this practice.

We think of the numerous examples throughout Scripture when people prayed and we see miracles happening. At times, though, prayers are not answered, such as the thorn in Paul's side.

> So to keep me from becoming conceited because of the surpassing greatness of the revelations, a thorn was given me in the flesh, a messenger of Satan to harass me, to keep me from becoming conceited. Three times I pleaded with the Lord about this, that it should leave me. But he said to me, "My grace is sufficient for you, for my power is made perfect in weakness." Therefore I will boast all the more gladly of my weaknesses, so that the power of Christ may rest upon me. For the sake of Christ, then, I am content with weaknesses, insults, hardships, persecutions, and calamities. For when I am weak, then I am strong. (2 Corinthians 12:7–10)

We may wonder why Paul only prayed three times. Why didn't he continue to plead with the Lord? How many times have we gone before the Lord and begged him for the same thing time and time again?

But God answered Paul. It wasn't the nice answer of "sure, if that's what you want, I'll make the pain go away." Instead, this answer helped Paul see the value of this trial. He almost became grateful for it because he knew that it was being used by God to grow him and prevent him from slipping into sin.

We may find it hard to relate to this, but if God continues to deny the requests of our prayer, we can pray a new prayer. We can ask him to help us to be content in the struggles and weaknesses. Our prayers can transform into prayers for contentment and gratitude for what we do have and for peace and joy in the midst of our suffering. This, too, grows us and teaches us to live in accordance with his will.

Of course, at times, our prayers will be answered, and we will have a wonderful testimony. In another occasion in 1 Corinthians, we read of answered prayers that benefited Paul in ways that he hoped for.

> For we do not want you to be unaware, brothers, of the affliction we experienced in Asia. For we were so utterly burdened beyond our strength that we despaired of life itself. Indeed, we felt that we had received the sentence of death. But that was to make us rely not on ourselves but on God who raises the dead. He delivered us from such a deadly peril, and he will deliver us. On him we have set our hope that he will deliver us again. You also must help us by prayer, so that many will give thanks on our behalf for the blessing granted us through the prayers of many. (2 Corinthians 1:8–11)

Here, Paul was delivered from torment and asks the church in Corinth to continue praying for them as they continue to find themselves in dangerous, precarious positions as they seek to spread the gospel.

Peter experienced another miracle when the prayers of the church were answered.

> So Peter was kept in prison, but earnest prayer for him was made to God by the church.
> Now when Herod was about to bring him out, on that very night, Peter was sleeping between two soldiers, bound with two chains, and sentries before the door were guarding the prison. And behold, an angel of the Lord stood next to him, and a light shone in the cell. He struck Peter on the side

and woke him, saying,"Get up quickly." And the chains fell off his hands. (Acts 12:5–7)

The funny part of this story is that people were praying for the release of Peter. When Peter was released, he went to their home, and when Tabitha answered the door, she slammed it in his face and told the others. And while they were praying for his release, they told her she was wrong.

Even when we pray for miracles, we struggle to accept these miracles as well. We have to trust and have faith that God will answer our prayers. He isn't bound by our faith, and he will answer based on his will, but if we are going to take the step of faith to pray, we should also believe when they are answered.

These big prayers about big matters are important. We should never feel that any prayer is too big or too small to bring before the Lord. We can fall on our faces before him, day after day, for hours at a time. But praying throughout the day is another important practice.

Instead of confining prayer to specific times or places, incorporating it into daily activities can foster a continual relationship with God. Again, simple prayers work well. If traffic is good on the way to work, say a quick prayer, thanking God. If you see a problem person, pray for God to save them.

I call these sharpshooting prayers: small, specific prayers offered in moments of need or gratitude. These brief, focused prayers can be a way of thanking God for everyday blessings or asking for help in particular situations. It's not the irreverent, casual praying I warned against but acknowledging that every moment gives us a chance to come before the Lord and petition him for whatever may be going on in our lives. It's a chance to thank him for every little thing, no matter how insignificant it may seem.

This practice can also involve directly praying with or for someone, offering them comfort, strength, and encouragement. One of the key principles of effective prayer is not asking for permission but simply doing it. We don't need to awkwardly seek approval before we pray.

This proactive approach encourages individuals to take initiative in their spiritual lives. Rather than hesitating or doubting their ability to pray, they are encouraged to act with confidence and trust in the power of prayer.

Inviting God into another's life and expecting an outcome is a demonstration of faith. This expectation is not about demanding specific results but about trusting God will respond in a meaningful way.

Prayer for healing is a specific type of intercessory prayer that seeks physical, emotional, or spiritual restoration. This practice is grounded in knowing God has the power to heal and transform. But we have to show this in our lives. Like Mary above, we pray a simple prayer. "Be healed, in Jesus's name." Then, we see if the healing took place, and we trust him in the process. Whether or not he heals in that moment is up to him. Our responsibility is to have the faith to believe he can heal.[64]

Daniel 3:16–18 gives us a prime example of the three stages of faith in our prayers.

> Shadrach, Meshach, and Abednego answered and said to the king, "O Nebuchadnezzar, we have no need to answer you in this matter. If this be so, our God whom we serve is able to deliver us from the burning fiery furnace, and he will deliver us out of your hand, O king. But if not, be it known to you, O king, that we will not serve your gods or worship the golden image that you have set up."

What are the three stages of faith demonstrated here?

1. God can
2. God will
3. But if not . . .

We must have faith that God can answer our prayers. We must have faith God will answer our prayers. And we must have faith that if God doesn't answer our prayers, he is still good and will still turn our pain for his glory and our good (Romans 8:28).

People lose their boldness when they feel the prayer was not answered. This could happen for several reasons. We could be praying against the unconditional will of God. We know that God wants people healed, but we don't know when or how he wants it

---

[64] To learn more about effective healing prayers, see Art Thomas's ministry at www.ArtThomas.org and www.SupernaturalTruth.com.

done. He may want someone else to pray for healing. He may want you to do it. We don't know what it could be. We do know that God heals, and we must ask.

There were zero times in the Bible that Jesus did not heal anyone that asked. In fact, when Jesus is approached by multitudes, it says, they all were healed.65 Not 79 percent, not all but one.

All (Matthew 15:29–39).

But then we wonder why Jesus only healed one person at the pool of Bethesda? What about the others who were sick? I cannot say why he picked the few, but we can say it was clear that the ones he did not heal did not ask.

We have the Holy Spirit working within us, but sadly, we have enough of the world in us to prevent us from having the perfect faith of Jesus. Our faith is limited, but our God is not. That should always be a source of comfort, knowing our weakness can't hinder his strength.

Praying for healing is a massive way to be bold. Let others see it and try to stop it. They can't. Only God determines our healing.

A Time for Boldness

Praying openly in response to danger is an expression of faith and courage. In times of crisis, public prayer can serve as a powerful witness to the strength and resilience of the faith community. It also provides collective support and solidarity, reminding individuals they are not alone in their struggles.

We learned this in a unique way at one of our restaurants shortly after the White Lives Matter rally that caused chaos in Charlottesville. The movement was coming to nearby Shelbyville and then on to our own Murfreesboro. They received permission to rally their protests, and a whole lot of groups planned to come along the way. Antifa and counter-protestors were coming, and all sorts of activity was expected. In Murfreesboro, we knew this could end up with a similar bedlam to that in Virginia.

Many local businesses boarded up their windows and armed

---

65 Our faith level doesn't determine whether or not Jesus can heal. For instance, if we don't have enough faith, that doesn't render Him incapable. He could still heal us. But our lack of faith may prevent us from asking for that healing or from asking with a genuine heart.

themselves, and other people simply did their best to stay indoors and avoid whatever consequences might arise from such hate-filled groups. Lots of local employees went out of state, leaving businesses short-staffed anyway. We, however, decided to take a different approach.

The group made their way through Shelbyville, and we waited for their arrival. Since we knew about how long it would probably take them to arrive on our doorstep, we were ready. We decided the best thing we could do wasn't to board the windows or load extra magazines like many others did. Instead, our calling was to pray.

About thirty minutes before the event was set to begin, we stopped the machine of our restaurant. We offered anyone who wanted to join us to come outside and pray. I expected maybe four or five people to respond. I never anticipated we would have at least fifty. In fact, so many people came to pray that some were actually still in the lobby of the restaurant because we didn't have enough space just outside the doors.

We opened in prayer, praying for whatever might hinder the arrival of these people. We prayed for rain and wind. We prayed for flat tires—after all, God got rid of the chariot wheels of the Egyptians, didn't he? Why couldn't he do the same to these people? And when we prayed for problems like flat tires, we prayed that a Christian might come along to help them fix it, someone who might be willing to stop and share the gospel even with hate-filled hearts.

That night, there was peace in Murfreesboro. No protestors arrived from White Lives Matter. No one showed up to follow through with the protest the city had approved.[66]

They were at Shelbyville, a thirty-minute drive down one street but then claimed they didn't know if they were welcome in our city or not. The truth is that we know for certain they intended to come. The night before, the police had found and confiscated tons of bottles of urine, bricks, and more. They found significant evidence that chaos was going to rain down on our town. But they never showed up.

A few news pieces reported what had happened—or hadn't, for that matter. At first, the claim was that the group was confused and

---

[66] Eric Levenson, "White Nationalists Cancel second rally in Tennessee," October 29, 2017, CNN, https://www.cnn.com/2017/10/28/us/tennessee-white-nationalist-rally-shelbyville-murfreesboro/index.html.

didn't know what to do, but they had their rally in Shelbyville and knew what to do there.

The news didn't cover our prayer, but we shared a video of it on Facebook, and it went viral. We only shared a small clip—a part of the prayer prayed by our prep cook trainer, the same young man who reminded me that Scripture is in our hearts where no one can take it away.

Prayer works. Many times, we don't recognize that, but that doesn't make it any less effective. The beauty of prayer is that it may be on our lips, but it is not in our hands. Our prayers rest in the hands of the One who can answer them with a yes, a no, or a not yet.

Be bold when you pray. Pray with faith, pray with humility, and pray diligently.

For Reflection

1. What do you think it means to pray with boldness? How is this different from simply praying out of habit or convenience? What does it look like to approach God with confidence, knowing he hears and responds to your prayers?

2. Why do you think many Christians struggle with praying out loud in front of others? How can you build confidence in public prayer, trusting that God honors your obedience and the opportunity to bless others through prayer?

3. The chapter mentions that we should pray with "reverence and humility." What does it mean to approach God in prayer with humility, and how does that affect the way we pray? How does humility shape the tone of your prayers, and how can it help you align your heart with God's will rather than your own desires?

4. The text discusses two extremes: praying with the belief that God will always answer our prayers if we have enough faith and dismissing prayer altogether because of God's sovereignty. Which of these extremes have you struggled with? How can we find a balanced perspective?

5. The story of Shadrach, Meshach, and Abednego illustrates three stages of faith: God can, God will, but if not.... Reflect on a time when you had to pray with these stages of faith in mind. How did it affect your prayer and trust in God's sovereignty?

6. The chapter emphasizes the importance of "sharpshooting prayers" or quick, specific prayers throughout the day. What are some ways you can integrate more spontaneous prayer into your daily routine? How does this practice help you stay connected with God in the midst of everyday life, strengthening your relationship with Him?

CHAPTER EIGHTEEN

Participate in Church

One of the many ways to help build your boldness is by attending church. This doesn't mean that if you go to church, you will suddenly become bold, but failing to go to church will definitely make you less bold. Without the stability of a church life, you stand alone. Standing alone generally leads to weariness.

We see that with the great prophet Elijah. After he brings the fires down from heaven, kills the prophets of Baal, and outruns a chariot, he then gets scared by a simple threat because he felt all alone. God had to show him how to navigate his way through this.

Something is intrinsically comforting about being around people with a like mind, direction, and purpose. Attending church means being part of a family that helps encourage and strengthen you. It helps your family to be strengthened as well, giving you a community to lean into when life is difficult or when you need help. It is worth every moment.

Going to church helps build confidence. You recognize you are not alone when the world tries to convince you that you are. When society says you're the one in the wrong, it's easier to believe them if you don't have others backing you up. But with a whole church community, you gain reassurance of your understanding of Scripture and truth.

What happens when you have a church backing you up?

And when he had come to Jerusalem, he [Paul] attempted to join the disciples. And they were all afraid of him, for they did not believe that he was a disciple. But Barnabas took him and brought him to the apostles and declared to them how on the road he had seen the Lord, who spoke to him, and how at Damascus he had preached boldly in the name of Jesus. So he went in and out among them at Jerusalem, preaching boldly in the name of the Lord. And he spoke and disputed against the Hellenists. But they were seeking to kill him. And when the brothers learned this, they brought him down to Caesarea and sent him off to Tarsus.

So the church throughout all Judea and Galilee and Samaria had peace and was being built up. And walking in the fear of the Lord and in the comfort of the Holy Spirit, it multiplied. (Acts 9:26–31)

For a man like Paul, who had persecuted the early church relentlessly and even participated in the deaths of martyrs, you may understand why the others in the church hesitated to welcome him. But it only took one man, one fellow believer, to convince the others to give Paul a chance and to speak on his behalf. The other disciples welcomed Paul so that as soon as he was in danger for preaching the truth himself, they came to rescue him and take him to safety so he could continue preaching faithfully.

This section is interesting as it tells how they brought Paul into the fold, but it's also counter-cultural to the frequent stories we hear today about those who deconstruct in their faith. So many American adults went to church as adolescents and claimed to be Christians. But it only took one or two bad interactions for them to turn from Christianity and deconstruct. That's similar to who I was before I met the person of the Holy Spirit.

Some women felt so shamed by purity culture that it caused problems in their marriage. They had been promised their obedience would lead to a loving, fulfilling life with their husbands. Thus, some choose premarital sexual activity over their faith because they think walking away from the church is the only way to escape the shame of their actions.

Some young men walked away from the church because they

were nerdy and didn't quite live up to the barely-an-adult-himself youth pastor's idea of cool. Therefore, they felt isolated and not one of the guys.

Meanwhile, those who understood their faith was not built upon the people in the church but rather on Christ tell very different stories. Some young women were abused by pastors and still attend church and still declare their faith in Jesus after taking a stand and calling these leaders out.

Of course, no church is perfect. The people in church are not perfect. The church community is full of sinners and hypocrites who will inevitably make mistakes. But these men who welcomed Paul knew their faith wasn't built on whether or not Paul might be trying to trick them. It didn't ultimately matter if their lives were threatened. (And we have already covered the fact that most of the original disciples died as martyrs.) They knew Christ was their foundation.

In the modern American church, we may have unpleasant moments, and we may feel the need to avoid certain people from Sunday to Sunday. Unfortunately, it's part of life.

But stopping church attendance altogether? Missing out on the opportunity to continue building a relationship with Jesus while allied with others who understand the source of their faith? That would be devastating.

In some sections of the country and in many parts of the world, going to church is made fun of. By doing so anyway, you are showing boldness. You are taking a stand just by attending and fearlessly letting people know you attend. This relates to what we looked at with the possibility of conflict: People won't necessarily respond well to your church attendance. But that doesn't matter. The reasons to go greatly outweigh the reasons to avoid church.

Church also charges you up for the week. Think about your cell phone. You need to plug it in to get through the day—maybe more than once if it's an older phone. If you don't charge it, eventually, your phone battery will die, and it becomes utterly useless. The same goes for Christians and the church.

The Bible stresses the importance of the Sabbath as a day of rest to recharge for the work ahead of us. But on that Sabbath day of rest, church attendance refuels us for whatever we may be walking into the next week. Will it be a week of weariness? Are you facing a difficult situation? Are you dealing with a boss who belittles and micromanages you? Are you a working mom who is also trying to raise children, and you just don't have the patience or energy for both? Are you grieving due to the loss of a family member or friend and have funeral arrangements to worry about?

Don't skip church. You need it. You need the reminder of how to forgive that boss and to know that your identity is not in your job. You're working for Jesus, not for a company. You need a reminder of peace from the anxiety that comes with imbalance. You need to understand the rest found in Christ and that you can lean on him to be patient with your children and enjoy them rather than stressing about their needs when you also have work to do.

You need the reminder that this life is not the end. The person you lost was hopefully a believer who is now in heaven. And, if not, you need the reminder to be bold in your relationships and to pray for others to come to know Jesus before it's too late. You need to remember your eternity is in God's hands and he is your strength and salvation.

Church gives us all these things through the peace of the music portion, through the Scripture preached from the pulpit, and through the relationships built with those who understand your pain and have compassion for you. It's a place to come as you are and to leave stronger through his grace.

Unfortunately, that may not be your experience with church. If you don't get that from your church, then you need to pray and ask the Holy Spirit to show you a church with that type of community. Your church might preach a shallow, feel-good message that tells you how to be a better person and to just live in a way that makes you happy. But that is not a good church.

If your church isn't preaching about the work Christ has accomplished on the cross for you to have a right relationship with God, it's more important than ever to start testing their preaching against the Bible. You shouldn't be leaving church with a to-do list thinking about yourself. You should leave church focusing on God, on what Jesus has done, and on how the Holy Spirit is working to draw you closer to him.

The people in your church, despite the fact that none are perfect and there will always be personality conflicts here and there, should be a source of encouragement and strength. They should be available to talk when life is hard and ready to celebrate the happy events.

Again, we see in the book of Acts just how important this community was.

> When he came and saw the grace of God, he was glad, and he exhorted them all to remain faithful to the Lord with steadfast purpose, for he was a good man, full of the Holy Spirit and of faith. And a great many people were added to the Lord. So Barnabas went to Tarsus to look for Saul, and when he had found him, he brought him to Antioch. For a whole year they met with the church and taught a great many people. And in Antioch the disciples were first called Christians.
>
> Now in these days prophets came down from Jerusalem to Antioch. And one of them named Agabus stood up and foretold by the Spirit that there would be a great famine over all the world (this took place in the days of Claudius). So the disciples determined, every one according to his ability, to send relief to the brothers living in Judea. And they did so, sending it to the elders by the hand of Barnabas and Saul. (Acts 11:23–30)

I have also been around many people who I know attend church, but they will not talk about it with their friends. For some reason, they don't feel comfortable sharing this aspect of their lives. Whether they think it will create conflict or one of the other multitude of reasons we covered in the first half of this book, they decide to keep their mouths shut about their experience with church as a Christian.

It does require a step of faith to show others that your strength is rooted in Christ. But it can easily be as simple as talking about something that happened in church with those who don't go. It doesn't take much to reach people and let them know you are a churchgoer. And you don't need to be ashamed of it. After all, if you are rooted in Christ, you will surely see church attendance as a gift.

When you start speaking about your church attendance, you will probably hear comments like, "I can get you out of the cult," or a rather sarcastic, "Say a prayer for me." But when those friends need help in times of trouble, they will turn to you. When they want to know more about Jesus, they won't ask their pagan friends. Instead, they will ask you to counsel them.

Your honesty will go a long way, and if they know that church is important to you, they are far more likely to understand that you're willing to talk through matters with them. They may start the conversation by saying they don't want to hear any of that church stuff, but if they can see that you have a peace they don't have, they're more inclined to turn to you for help. At that point, you can be honest and tell them you understand they don't want to hear about Christianity, but they will not find peace or freedom in a source outside that. Tell them truthfully that if they're looking for help or how to have your peace, that's the only answer you can give.

Trust and Another Boldness

Your boldness is also reflected in your generosity with money. In today's economy, many people probably don't want to hear about this. If giving is not already part of your lifestyle, it may feel like the last thing you want to talk about. It may be an area of faith you'd rather shrug off and ignore.

After all, we think, "what if their budget puts $20,000 a year toward the sound equipment and only $15,000 toward missionaries?"

There are many books and articles on this, and you can do your own research. The Holy Spirit will lead and convict you in the areas needed. I'm not here to teach about the breakdown of tithe, just to encourage this act of faith, obedience, and boldness as we are instructed by Scripture.

But giving generously is not about earning a reward. It is an act of trust, obedience, and worship. No, it's not always comfortable or convenient, but it is biblical.

So often, we get bogged down in questions. How much should I give? Should it go to my church, a missionary, or a charity? What if leaders spend it on things I don't agree with? These questions can distract us from the bigger issue. At its core, generosity isn't about percentages or accounting. It's about whether we trust God enough to release what is already His.

The truth is this: it is all God's money. Every cent. He has entrusted it to us to steward well, and part of that stewardship is to give freely and sacrificially. The church and other ministries are responsible before God for how they use those gifts. But we are responsible for whether or not we gave them with open hands and faithful hearts. Charles Stanley says, "God is responsible for the consequences of our obedience. We are responsible for the consequences of our disobedience."

Generosity stretches us. When I am tempted to justify giving less, I make myself give more. Not because God needs it, but because my heart does. I don't want to let selfishness take root. Generosity guards against that.

I remember when I was not a Christian but occasionally went to church. I would drop in a small amount, just enough to look like I had done something. It wasn't a sacrifice. It wasn't obedience. It was for me, and what others thought of me. It was not for God. I didn't want others to see what I was not doing, so I had to do something, but they didn't see the amount I hidden in the envelope. Looking back, this was a pathetic way of thinking.

It is bold to give generously. When you choose to let go of what you could keep for yourself, you fortify your character and declare your trust in God. You are saying with your actions, "I believe He will provide for me, even when it costs me something." After all, everything you already have is from Him.

"Remember this: Whoever sows sparingly will also reap sparingly, and whoever sows generously will also reap generously. Each of you should give what you have decided in your heart to give, not reluctantly or under compulsion, for God loves a cheerful giver." (2 Cor. 9:6–7)

This kind of giving builds resilience and inner strength. It transforms us. It reminds us that the things of this world are temporary and that eternal investments matter most. God will use our sacrifice in ways we may never see. People will be blessed, ministries will flourish, and the kingdom will advance.

When you doubt whether generosity really matters, remember all the ways God has already sustained you. If you pray but rarely give, it's time to start. If you attend church but never support it financially, it's time to invest. If you feel the sting of sacrifice, thank God for the chance to live by faith.

Our boldness matters. And one of the boldest steps we can take is to give generously, trusting that God will use it for His purposes.

For Reflection

1. How has your church attendance affected your spiritual boldness? How does regular church attendance affect your sense of peace and confidence as you live out your faith?

2. The chapter describes Elijah loneliness despite great victories. Have you ever experienced a similar feeling of weariness or fear when you felt isolated in your faith? How did God or your church community help you during that time?

3. The chapter mentions Paul's boldness in preaching after receiving support from other believers. How can sharing your church experiences with others serve as a form of bold testimony? What might prevent you from being open about your testimony, and how can you overcome these obstacles to inspire others?

4. Why do you think some people deconstruct their faith after negative experiences in church? How can your church community offer support and healing to those struggling with doubts or negative experiences in their spiritual journey?

5. The chapter acknowledges that no church is perfect and people may disappoint us. How do you reconcile the imperfections of the church with your call to remain a part of it and to contribute to its growth and healing?

6. How does consistently attending church and tithing help you build spiritual resilience and discipline? How do these consistent practices strengthen your faith and help you persevere through life's challenges?

7. What do you think about the idea of being bold just by showing up to church in a society that often ridicules or dismisses religious practices? How can we stand firm in our faith when the world is hostile to Christianity?

8. The chapter talks about how to deal with churches that may not align with your beliefs, especially in terms of preaching. How can

you discern whether to stay and work for change or to seek a church that more closely aligns with your beliefs?

CHAPTER NINETEEN

Forgive

We covered quite a bit about forgiveness while discussing the obstacles to boldness, especially when we looked at compassion and the importance of forgiving those who don't show it. But there's more to cover on this topic, especially if we are truly going to make a difference in the world and with our boldness.

It's important to acknowledge the very act of forgiveness requires a boldness not of our own making. We have no choice but to lean on God and trust in Him if we are going to show forgiveness toward others. It is so easy to withhold mercy when we feel our rights are being stripped away or that others are treating us unjustly.

As we have seen throughout the past few years and as addressed in this book, many events are happening that make us feel that way. Our rights are being stripped away. We are being treated unjustly. We looked at three stories in the first chapter of people who were unfairly persecuted for standing up for their faith.

So many Christians in America and the West today consider us on the slippery slope of intense persecution. And while it's true that there are many signs this will only get worse, we also need to have perspective of just how fortunate we still are. We have to be aware of how many rights we do still have for now. Even the fact that I'm allowed to write this book and you are allowed to read is evidence we have not been so badly impacted by injustice that we've lost all our freedoms.

The freedom to forgive is an important value, and the act of boldness will maintain those freedoms. Stand up when you need to, show mercy when you need to, and don't back down.

Yes, it really is easy to withhold mercy when we face struggles, but that doesn't require any boldness at all. That only leaves us feeling as empty as anyone else. Ultimately, the only people harmed by our lack of forgiveness are ourselves. Unforgiveness grows into bitterness and seeps deeply into our hearts.

But we live in a culture of victim mindsets and hurt. We want to be wounded. The trend of young adults cutting off communication with their parents is often accompanied by the words *toxic* and *narcissistic* if the parents don't affirm every single lifestyle choice the child makes. And as we just looked at, even Christians can lean into the persecuted mindset when, in reality, the Bible actually said that would eventually happen.

When this victimhood is the cultural norm for vastly different people groups, how can we expect people to boldly forgive and offer mercy toward those who have hurt them? Forgiveness seems to be the very antithesis of what we expect from one another.

But we can't just assign the lack of forgiveness to our modern day and the entitlement culture we live in. If people hadn't always struggled with forgiveness, there would have been no reason for the Bible to even address the issue.

The fact that humans are naturally sinful means we can remain confident that the same sins we see today have existed throughout history and will probably not change or disappear. We may just change the mechanisms we use. For example, we move from temple prostitutes to online pornography. Sin is sin, and it's ever present in a fallen world.

We can also acknowledge that despite the fact that our sinful hearts don't want to offer forgiveness, people outside Christianity still do sometimes choose to forgive. At least, they offer a form of it, particularly when they lean into a vaguely spiritual worldview or one that values their own psychology and healing journey.

Gandhi said, "The weak can never forgive. Forgiveness is the attribute of the strong."[67] While this may be true from a secular perspective and wise in the eyes of the world, as Christians, we know that forgiveness is the attribute of Christ, and our strength rests entirely in him. We are incapable of fully healing and forgiving without him.

From the world's point of view, it makes sense to forgive because we don't want to stay hurt or retain the bitterness. It also makes us feel better about ourselves when we show mercy toward someone else because it immediately elevates us, making us feel like we're better than they are. But is it truly forgiveness if we do it for purely selfish motives? Are there different levels of forgiveness? Can we truly forgive outside of Christ, or are we simply suppressing our feelings and trying to "just move on"?

Historically, at many times, people have chosen to forgive to some extent, no matter their worldview. But as we are looking at this from a perspective of boldness in Christ, we have to hold to the real foundation of where forgiveness comes from and what it means for us as believers.

In chapter 10, discussing this issue and the lack of compassion, we examined the parable of the unforgiving servant in Matthew 18. This is the foundation of forgiveness. This is what it means to show mercy. Through the work of Jesus on the cross, we have been forgiven much. As a result, we can forgive the comparatively little offenses (no matter how large they may be) that have been committed against us.

While culture shifts and shame fades, sins may become more or less prominent as time goes on. But it doesn't change the reality that sin has always been and always will be around.

Forgiveness is the same. At times, we don't want to forgive. At times, we don't want to let go of the hurts that have been inflicted upon us. But if we are unwilling to forgive, we are unwilling to obey God's instructions. The lack of forgiveness is active sin.

However, a key component to forgiveness is often overlooked when it's accessible. Depending on the circumstances, you may not be able to speak with the person who hurt you. You could be letting go of a hurt from a deceased parent or someone who is no longer in your life. Maybe a classmate was particularly cruel to you in high

---

[67] Mahatma Gandhi, *All Men Are Brothers* (Bloomsbury Academic, 2005), 166. According to this book, Gandhi originally stated this in 1931.

school and they had an extremely generic name, so you can't even track them down on social media.

But whenever possible, it's important to tell the offender that you forgive them. There is value in boldly showing them mercy even if they haven't asked for it and even if they aren't repentant. And then, you need to tell them why. You don't forgive because you're a nice person. You don't forgive because you're a doormat and you think it's okay to let people treat you poorly or walk all over you.

The offender needs to know you are forgiving them because God forgave you. You are forgiving them because God commands it. It is to your benefit to let go and be free of the pain and bitterness, but you ultimately forgive so that you can live obediently and boldly for Christ.

In the parable of the unforgiving servant, the master made it clear to the servant that he was being punished because he hadn't shown a lesser mercy to someone else even after he'd been shown such an incredible mercy. So when we are forgiving others, they need to understand we aren't doing so out of a grand gesture to prove how much better we are than them. We're doing it out of the humility of knowing we have been forgiven for much greater sins.

When you tell other people they are forgiven for what they've done to you, it shouldn't be with any great expectation. They might be deeply apologetic and grateful for your mercy. But they might laugh or scoff at you, thinking they did nothing wrong, or that you deserved what they did to you. Forgiveness born out of expectation is not true forgiveness either.

Jesus died for the salvation of mankind, yet we still see scoffers everywhere. Some flaunt their sin, even using it to mock Jesus himself as we have seen with religious-themed drag shows over the past few years. If the Creator and Savior of the universe can handle being mocked, it shouldn't be a problem for us.

Whatever one's theological view may be—that only those whom he predestined will ultimately turn to him or that salvation is open to all who freely choose to turn to him—it doesn't change the reality that Jesus came to save sinners. He has offered salvation to all. And despite that mercy, people still respond in such a grotesque way.

If, in their sin, humans can treat their only true rescue with such contempt, we shouldn't be surprised when they respond similarly toward us when we offer forgiveness. As nice as it would be to have a response of gratitude and apology, that's just not always how it goes.

Sometimes we are met with excuses and embarrassment; sometimes, with sheer hatred. But bold forgiveness and bold declarations of what Christ has done for us are still the answer.

Don't let yourself get caught up in uncertainty or discomfort because you don't know how to forgive and move on without letting someone hurt you all over again. You are demonstrating vulnerability, and that's okay. You can still be strong and set boundaries where necessary, but fear shouldn't stop us from forgiving. Lean on Christ as your strength and let go of what others have done.

For Reflection

1. Consider how the act of forgiveness often requires a boldness that comes from God, not from ourselves. Reflect on a time when you found it difficult to forgive and how God's strength helped you let go of that hurt.

2. Reflect on a situation where unforgiveness affected you. How did it impact your peace, relationships, and spiritual life? How does releasing unforgiveness bring healing and freedom?

3. Consider how the victim mentality contrasts with the call to forgive boldly. What are some practical ways you can choose to forgive, even when the culture encourages holding onto hurt or resentment?

4. Reflect on the distinction between secular forgiveness, which might be more about suppressing negative feelings, and biblical forgiveness, which involves releasing others and trusting God. How does Christ's forgiveness of us shape our ability to forgive others?

5. The chapter emphasizes that forgiveness is an act of obedience, not just an emotional release. How does viewing forgiveness as obedience to God change the way you approach the act of forgiving?

6. What does it mean to forgive without any expectation of the other person's response? Why is it important not to expect an apology or change in behavior when we offer forgiveness?

7. In a culture that often encourages resentment, division, and holding grudges, what are some challenges you face in offering forgiveness to others? How can you overcome those challenges?

8. Reflect on Christ's ultimate act of forgiveness, especially as he was mocked and scorned. How can his willingness to forgive even those who rejected him inspire you to forgive others, especially when they respond with indifference or hostility?

CHAPTER TWENTY

Stand Up Against Culture

Taking a stand against culture tends to be one of the hardest things for us to do. At the same time, this is the top response from most people when I ask them what boldness looks like. People must stand up against culture.

Everything we have discussed so far has been a foundation for boldness. We must stand up against the world's culture because we are not of this world. By living antithetically to the things of the world, we are naturally shunning what is not of Christ. But there is a difference between avoidance and obedience. Avoidance is not boldness.

One trend is the cultural exit: leaving society and moving to the country to homeschool, homestead, and reject the powers that be. Likewise, many people have decided to quit social media and delete their accounts.

None of these things are bad. They're great if done for the right reasons, like raising a mentally, physically, and spiritually healthy family or to find peace instead of anxiety. But these actions are not boldness, and they are not necessarily the answer to standing up against culture.

Yes, maybe you live in an area where homeschooling really is an act of boldness and a way to stand up against what's being done in your local schools. But if you're going to take that step, speak out as to why. Don't hesitate to make it known you are leaving these circumstances because you believe what's being done in schools is wrong.

You cannot shield your family from the sin of the world, so don't even try. Protecting innocence is a worthy endeavor, but attempting to escape and hide from what's going on in the world won't create any sort of impact for the kingdom of God.

While avoidance and belligerence look very different in action, they are both adjacent to boldness. One is a fearful escapism that makes us look weak. The other is an obnoxious, pushy ranting against culture that makes Christians appear unhinged. In contrast, in boldness, we can stand firm, make the right decisions for ourselves and our families, speak up, and ultimately expose hard hearts to merciful truths.

What does this practically look like for you in your circumstance? Only you can answer that, but you will need to seek the wisdom of Scripture as you do. Again, a church family or trusted pastor can also help you discover what the best steps are.

On the whole, however, we can follow a few principles in how we engage others as we make strides to be bold and stand up against culture.

We are designed for one-on-one interactions with others as we make our stand, but we need to take this boldness to a much higher level if we plan on being an ambassador for Christ. In addition to our one-on-one encounters, we can stand up and stand out whenever needed, sharing the good news of the kingdom and making disciples in all nations—including the one we live in.

You may not have a huge platform, and that's perfectly fine. Sure, it would be great if YouTube or Rumble were flooded by Christians taking a stand. But ultimately, the belligerent would turn everyone's comment sections into theological debates while unbelievers would troll them.

Some people will have a platform and take a stand on social media. I'm grateful for my podcast, where I've had guests with whom I agree and those whom I am less inclined to support. But not everyone is meant to go that route.

Your platform may be as a business owner with a small team. Whether or not your employees are Christians, you start the day with a prayer and reading a section of Scripture. Maybe you're a teacher and you refuse to bow to gender ideology with your students even if it means losing your job.

Taking a stand matters. You never know who might need to see it. Take the three people we mentioned earlier in the book. They probably did not realize their stance would be seen and discussed across the nation and world. In this day and age, one person with a phone can make information go viral. The same is true when you choose *not* to take a stand.

Others might have chosen to dwell in the avoidance arena, but upon seeing your boldness, they no longer want to hide. Or someone could be quite confused, and they just don't know what to believe. But seeing your willingness to lose it all has given them the courage to look into Christianity even when their friends mock them for it.

Whatever your platform looks like and whatever form your stand takes, this boldness is critical in demonstrating a true, just faith that seeks the glory of God's kingdom on earth. We can't let the loud, belligerent voices of our enemies drown us out. We cannot allow the wicked to be more passionate in the defense of their beliefs than we are in the name of truth.

As John Calvin said, "A dog barks when his master is attacked. I would be a coward if I saw that God's truth is attacked and yet would remain silent."[68] You may read this and think it's foolish. After all, if God is so grand, why does he even need our defense? Isn't he capable of defending himself? Sure, absolutely. God doesn't need our defense. He is all-powerful and sovereign. He can absolutely bring the earth to its knees and lead everyone in faithful worship of him. He can stand in his own right and has throughout the ages.

God allowed so many things to happen throughout Israel's history purely for the purpose of demonstrating his own glory and showing that he didn't actually need help from the people he used in those situations, such as Gideon and his army in Judges 7.

> The Lord said to Gideon, "The people with you are too many for me to give the Midianites into their hand, lest Israel boast over me, saying, 'My own hand has saved me.' Now therefore proclaim in the ears of the people, saying,

---

[68] George Sweeting, *Who Said That? More Than 2,500 Usable Quotes and Illustrations* (Moody Publishers, 1995).

'Whoever is fearful and trembling, let him return home and hurry away from Mount Gilead.'" Then 22,000 of the people returned, and 10,000 remained. (Judges 7:2–3)

God had no desire to hear His people boast that the army was victorious through their own strength. He chose to bring the army from thirty-two thousand to ten thousand.

But even this was too many.

And the Lord said to Gideon, "The people are still too many. Take them down to the water, and I will test them for you there, and anyone of whom I say to you, 'This one shall go with you,' shall go with you, and anyone of whom I say to you, 'This one shall not go with you,' shall not go." So he brought the people down to the water. And the Lord said to Gideon, "Every one who laps the water with his tongue, as a dog laps, you shall set by himself. Likewise, every one who kneels down to drink." And the number of those who lapped, putting their hands to their mouths, was 300 men, but all the rest of the people knelt down to drink water. And the Lord said to Gideon, "With the 300 men who lapped I will save you and give the Midianites into your hand, and let all the others go every man to his home." So the people took provisions in their hands, and their trumpets. And he sent all the rest of Israel every man to his tent, but retained the 300 men. And the camp of Midian was below him in the valley. (Judges 7:4–8)

God clearly didn't need Gideon or any of those men to fight. He could have done it himself. But he chose to use them and then used as few of them as possible just to prove that only he could have brought them victory.

Likewise, the story of David and Goliath demonstrates this (1 Samuel 17). True, many people read this as a tale where we fight our enemies (challenges), but in this story, we are the scared Israelites in need of a Savior. Amidst an army of Israelites, God used a mere shepherd boy with a stone against a giant villain. In the same way, Jesus has defeated the devil. Jesus came to earth through the humblest of circumstances and lived a life that would have been largely unimpressive were it not for his final years of ministry and the revelation that this fully man was also fully God.

The Bible is filled with stories that evidence the reality that God doesn't need us to fight for him. As Jesus reminded Peter in the garden, Jesus could bring the angels down if he wanted to.

> While he was still speaking, Judas came, one of the twelve, and with him a great crowd with swords and clubs, from the chief priests and the elders of the people. Now the betrayer had given them a sign, saying, "The one I will kiss is the man; seize him." And he came up to Jesus at once and said, "Greetings, Rabbi!" And he kissed him. Jesus said to him, "Friend, do what you came to do." Then they came up and laid hands on Jesus and seized him. And behold, one of those who were with Jesus stretched out his hand and drew his sword and struck the servant of the high priest and cut off his ear. Then Jesus said to him, "Put your sword back into its place. For all who take the sword will perish by the sword. Do you think that I cannot appeal to my Father, and he will at once send me more than twelve legions of angels? But how then should the Scriptures be fulfilled, that it must be so?" At that hour Jesus said to the crowds, "Have you come out as against a robber, with swords and clubs to capture me? Day after day I sat in the temple teaching, and you did not seize me. But all this has taken place that the Scriptures of the prophets might be fulfilled." Then all the disciples left him and fled. (Matthew 26:47–56)

With all these examples and more, we can easily admit that God doesn't need us to fight his battles. However, as we have already looked at and acknowledged, when people see us stepping out in faith anyway and see the risks we take in this world, they will start to ask about our boldness. Darkness does not like the light, but we are to shine our light in the darkness. We are to lean into the strength we have in Jesus in obedience.

God may not need our help to fight his battles, but he has called us to be faithful anyway. He has ordained that we should get uncomfortable. Maybe it is his sovereign will for us, or maybe it is for our own sake and growing in our faith. The truth is, we don't get to question why God wants us to be bold, even if he doesn't need our help. We just have to respond in obedience and be bold anyway.

A Crutch for the Weak

Before I became a Christian, I had a lot of issues with Christianity. I thought it seemed to be a crutch for weak people. They would say a lot about what they believed, but as soon as life became difficult, oftentimes because of me and my interactions with them, they would either get mad or shut down. I didn't see the power of the gospel. I didn't see Christians standing up against culture while also standing for what they believed. There was a lot of talk and not a whole lot of action.

When I was still pretty anti-Christian, I would try to make people cry about their Christian faith. I have to say, I was pretty successful at this most of the time. I had a great strategy that managed to break most people. I started by twisting their words and making them look stupid, then I would take verses out of context when necessary to prove my point. Sometimes, they would cuss and storm off, frustrated because they didn't have an adequate rebuttal. But that only made me laugh.

One guy had totaled his car. He was showing off the mangled mess he had survived, and there, on the front license plate, it said, God is my co-pilot. In my cynicism at the time, I replied in the only way I could. I quipped, "Looks like God wasn't there that day." As usual, I deployed sarcasm and bite so the other guy couldn't win. I used plain logic while this other guy responded in raw emotion and anger. It's easy to win a debate in a situation like that. When a Christian is already emotional and tends to be hot-headed or unprepared, they just get angry. I knew how to use that for my own benefit. It was easy to argue, and the angrier they got or the sooner they would cry, the better I felt about my justifications.

It's important to know the difference between what you were taught and what you understand. I knew how to push the buttons of what people were taught when their understanding was pitifully limited.

On occasion, people would stand up to me politely and kindly. I couldn't get a rise out of them, and they didn't take the bait. They would challenge me, and I really didn't like those people. It wasn't as fun if they didn't get riled up and upset.

But that was a long time ago, and I was a different person—

one who didn't know Christ. Now I get to use those experiences to help wake people up to the strategies and tactics so often used against us.

When Christians folded, caved in and didn't stand up, it added to the illusion that Christians are weak and can't do anything on their own—that they are using religion as a crutch. As a result, they seemed weak because many of them presented themselves that way.

After I finally met Jesus, one of the first questions I asked myself was "How would I respond to me?" I knew I would eventually have to face that. I knew many other people out there would behave the way I had, and they would now challenge me as I had done to others not so long ago.

What Now?

So how do we do it? How do we actively stand up against a culture that is so hostile toward our faith and our Savior?

First of all, when we see something wrong, we don't encourage it, laugh at it, or promote it. We don't make excuses, and we don't pretend we can stand adjacent to sin just because of convenience or any other excuse we covered in the first half of this book.

We think of Jaelene Daniels and her refusal to wear the pride jersey as a women's soccer player. But if we compare this to the acts of the Westboro Baptist Church who set up protests at the funerals of LGBT people, including those who have been murder victims, we see the stark contrast of boldness over belligerence.

Mocking someone's sinful lifestyle at their funeral does no one any benefit and only hurts the family and friends of those left behind. Shouts that the person is burning in hell won't turn anyone to Christ. It is a very different approach than someone simply upholding their own moral standard and choosing to step aside if that is the only option they have.

I know it is easier to be a bully than to be bullied. I have been a bully, and I've been bullied. That is the difference between being bold versus being belligerent.

In Los Angeles, a Christian lifeguard received partial accommodation to his request not to fly pride flags at the beach where he was working. However, without notice, the accommodation was removed. He has since claimed he was harassed for his beliefs and was discriminated against. He was even removed from his position.[69]

In my business, we faced an issue during the Black Lives Matter social media blitz when everyone was putting up black squares and making statements. We refused to engage in the social media trend. Our reason for refusing had nothing to do with our beliefs. Rather, we couldn't in good conscience represent the BLM organization. The sentiment that black lives matter is true in that the Bible is clear there is no Jew nor Greek, slave nor free, etc. "For as many of you as were baptized into Christ have put on Christ. There is neither Jew nor Greek, there is neither slave nor free, there is no male and female, for you are all one in Christ Jesus. And if you are Christ's, then you are Abraham's offspring, heirs according to promise." (Galatians 3:27–29). No one is more or less important because of their race.

But we couldn't associate with the organization itself, which is anti-Christian. Their views often directly oppose and contradict the Christian worldview, and they are clear they advocate for a society without Christ at the center.

This decision, however, caused problems at the restaurant, and we had no choice but to handle it. An angry employee started to rile up others because we didn't do more. All this employee wanted was for us to post a black background and white letters like everyone else.

It really didn't make an impact in my opinion. Was it supposed to make you no longer racist if you posted that? It's ridiculous to think social media has so much influence that you can allege that one small restaurant posting a black square would make a difference to people.

But whether it made a difference or not, we couldn't join the trend since an anti-Christian group was fueling it. Instead, I agreed to meet with every black employee who was willing. I gathered others to join us for a meeting, including our director of operations, my wife, and even my kids so that we could discuss and understand what was going on.

We scheduled the meeting and a small percentage showed up, maybe twenty people. One person called ahead who couldn't make it but they chatted through some of the specific issues about how we

---

[69] K. Parks and Fox News, "Lifeguard sues LA County, alleges he was punished for refusing to fly Progress Pride Flag," Fox News, May 31, 2024, https://www.foxnews.com/media/lifeguard-sues-la-county-alleges-punished-refusing-fly-progress-pride-flag.

ran the restaurant. I appreciated that feedback, which led to some changes, such as how we now celebrate Martin Luther King Day and specifically his Christian walk with many of his faith-filled quotes around the restaurant.

But in that meeting, I started by asking the people in the group what they wanted to be called—African Americans, black Americans, etc., and they couldn't agree. Everyone had a different view on the issue. I thought it was important to start with a baseline if we were going to address race. I was there to learn. I couldn't support an anti-Christian group, but that didn't mean I didn't want to know how we could better to support our employees.

Then, the one troublemaker started spouting false statements. I had to respond. I even found myself explaining my background and that I'm not even Caucasian—I'm Greek or Hellenic. Making assumptions about my background and ethnicity is wrong as well.

I was shocked by the lack of education and knowledge they had of black culture as well. I was a sociology major, specializing in race and ethnic relations. I volunteered with the NAACP for a while. This person was angry that I wouldn't post a black square and tried to get others riled up, but they knew nothing of my background or just how familiar I was with the work that had been and was still being done in their communities.

I'm not going to exploit and pander people or situations to make money. Instead, I read the aforementioned Galatians 3:29 and pointed out that we're all the same in Christ Jesus, and that's how we would operate. We never had a single problem after that. In fact, people thanked me for being there and for bringing my kids. I was willing to listen from a Christian perspective and explain why the black square went against my conscience.

To this employee, I needed to prove I was on their side. It's not as simple as that in reality, however. So often, we look at the things of the world and assume they trump truth and take priority. We have to start looking at the way God sees things. He doesn't sit around and wait or listen just to decide what's best. He knows exactly what's best for us and for this world.

A meaningless black square didn't represent any true understanding of what some people may experience due to their race. It represented an institution that opposes my view of God as a Christian. That was reason enough for me to reject it.

Speaking Out

We are to tell people when culture is wrong. If we don't know why it's wrong, then we have to find out. If we don't know why we disagree with gay marriage, we have to find out. If we don't know why we disagree with abortion, we have to find out. Remember that it's not about politics. It's about the truth of a holy and righteous God who determines right from wrong. But we must first act.

In his book *Tactics*, Greg Koukl suggests two primary questions when discussing our Christian convictions.

- What does that mean?
- How did you draw that conclusion?[70]

With that in mind, we have to start asking these questions.

One day, I was at Whole Foods, looking for a particular kind of cheese. Two people working there were having a friendly disagreement and one made a comment along the lines of, "I don't believe that any people should tell you whether your opinion is right or wrong."

The conversation was interesting, so I figured I'd join in. I asked what he meant by that statement. He tried to tell me that everyone has their own truth and that there's no such thing as absolute truth. It's a fairly common opinion these days, but this view has plenty of holes.

I followed up with some casual questions. I asked if math is true. Then I took it a step further. "Can I pay fifty cents for this block of cheese? That's how I see it, and you can't tell me it's wrong."

The guy said that truth is variable only on moral issues. Naturally, I asked if there's such a thing as morality. I asked him how he knew his morality is true. It was a friendly and engaging conversation, so I wasn't simply trying to poke the bear. I just wanted to get him thinking, and thankfully, it seemed to be working. These two employees were enjoying the chat as much as I was.

I didn't share my opinions, but I asked them about these

---

[70] Greg Koukl, *Tactics: A Game Plan for Discussing Your Christian Convictions* (Zondervan, 2009).

matters, and they finally admitted there had to be a Creator of moral order. They weren't ready to admit there is a God, and they didn't concede to a Christian viewpoint, but it was still a start. I prayed God would bring someone to continue those conversations with them individually, since I could only go so deep. But it was a great opportunity to open the door, and the employees were excited and said I could come back and talk any time.

Another time, I was able to have a similar conversation, looking at what it means and how we draw conclusions. I had a manager tell me she was pescatarian because she didn't think fish had souls. I asked about cows and dogs. Then I asked, "What is a soul?" She thinks cows and dogs do have souls, and we had an interesting discussion. This ultimately opened the door to a spiritual discussion that could be continued later.

How They Respond

We've looked at how the lack of confidence can stop us from being bold. The fear of not knowing the answers applies to unbelievers as well. They may be just as uncomfortable defending their viewpoints as we are.

Don't expect them to back down, even if they are insecure as to why they believe what they do. The point isn't to win our argument with them but to plant a seed and open the door for them to have later discussions that could open their eyes. Let someone else water the seed down the road. That might be the best approach. Sometimes it just seems so obvious that you are right and they are wrong.

But as my pastor has to remind me, when I say, "Can't you see . . . it means they can't." If I'm pointing out the obvious and they clearly don't get it, it means they need more patience, more grace, and more *from you*. They may need more time or another voice from someone else's perspective. When they laugh at you, go back to forgiveness. Who cares if they laugh? It has happened in the past, and it will happen in the future. In the end, it doesn't matter.

For Reflection

1. Consider why some Christians withdraw from mainstream culture through actions like leaving social media. How can these actions be helpful but also limiting if we see them as the only solution to cultural pressure?

2. What role does Scripture play in discerning when to take a stand against culture? Reflect on how Scripture guides you in making decisions about when to challenge cultural norms. How can you rely on God's Word to help you discern when to take a stand in boldness and when to show grace?

3. What are the potential dangers of being belligerent when standing up against culture, and how can we avoid falling into this trap? How can you stand firm in your beliefs without becoming arrogant, defensive, or unnecessarily antagonistic?

4. What does it mean to stand firm in the face of cultural pressure, and why is this concept important for a Christian without sounding arrogant or overly combative? How can you maintain humility and love while holding fast to your convictions in a hostile culture?

5. Why is it important to understand that boldness may not always require a public platform like social media? How can you stand firm in your convictions in smaller, more personal spaces even when you're not on a public stage?

6. Why does God call us to be bold, even when he doesn't need us to defend his truth? How does the story of Gideon's battle in Judges 7 illustrate this idea?

7. What are the dangers of only talking about faith without living it out, especially when facing opposition from the culture around us? How does living your faith boldly, even when opposed, make your words more credible and impactful in the eyes of others?

CHAPTER TWENTY-ONE

Use Money As Boldness

Love it or hate it, money seems to make the world go around. There never seems to be enough of it. We're never happy with how other people use it, and we rarely feel content with the amount we have in our own pockets. And while money doesn't bring happiness, it can certainly make life easier and less stressful. Because money is such a necessary part of daily life, we need to look at it from a biblical perspective while also acknowledging how it is relevant to this topic of boldness.

The way you use your money to stand up against culture is critical. Money is a gift from God, but it can also be a curse. God can bless us with money and make us prosperous. In those times, we are grateful we have what we need. God can also use the lack of money to teach us to depend on him. In those times, we may feel broken and anxious, but we must acknowledge God is still good in the midst of our trials.

Alternatively, having a lot of money can make us self-reliant, and not having money can make us bitter. We can really choose any number of attitudes and responses, depending on our circumstances.

But what does the Bible have to say about it? Deuteronomy gives us a number of examples to show us the value of a right attitude about our finances. From the importance of remembering that they are sourced by God alone to the principles of tithe, we can use this book as our guide.

First, we see where our provision comes from.

> The whole commandment that I command you today you shall be careful to do, that you may live and multiply, and go in and possess the land that the Lord swore to give to your fathers. And you shall remember the whole way that the Lord your God has led you these forty years in the wilderness, that he might humble you, testing you to know what was in your heart, whether you would keep his commandments or not. And he humbled you and let you hunger and fed you with manna, which you did not know, nor did your fathers know, that he might make you know that man does not live by bread alone, but man lives by every word that comes from the mouth of the Lord. Your clothing did not wear out on you and your foot did not swell these forty years. Know then in your heart that, as a man disciplines his son, the Lord your God disciplines you. So you shall keep the commandments of the Lord your God by walking in his ways and by fearing him. For the Lord your God is bringing you into a good land, a land of brooks of water, of fountains and springs, flowing out in the valleys and hills, a land of wheat and barley, of vines and fig trees and pomegranates, a land of olive trees and honey, a land in which you will eat bread without scarcity, in which you will lack nothing, a land whose stones are iron, and out of whose hills you can dig copper. And you shall eat and be full, and you shall bless the Lord your God for the good land he has given you. (Deuteronomy 8:1–10)

We see how incredibly God has provided for us and that everything we have is given to us by him. We see how God humbled the Israelites and how he provided for them even through the years in the desert.

But as they received prosperity, he warned them against the potential pitfalls.

> Take care lest you forget the Lord your God by not keeping his commandments and his rules and his statutes, which I command you today, lest, when you have eaten and are full

and have built good houses and live in them, and when your herds and flocks multiply and your silver and gold is multiplied and all that you have is multiplied, then your heart be lifted up, and you forget the Lord your God, who brought you out of the land of Egypt, out of the house of slavery, who led you through the great and terrifying wilderness, with its fiery serpents and scorpions and thirsty ground where there was no water, who brought you water out of the flinty rock, who fed you in the wilderness with manna that your fathers did not know, that he might humble you and test you, to do you good in the end. Beware lest you say in your heart, "My power and the might of my hand have gotten me this wealth." You shall remember the Lord your God, for it is he who gives you power to get wealth, that he may confirm his covenant that he swore to your fathers, as it is this day. And if you forget the Lord your God and go after other gods and serve them and worship them, I solemnly warn you today that you shall surely perish. Like the nations that the Lord makes to perish before you, so shall you perish, because you would not obey the voice of the Lord your God. (Deuteronomy 8:11–20)

Money is a blessing. But God warns Israel not to become too reliant on it or to believe that they achieved it. This is when we start believing in the god of self and start worshiping money.

We can't allow ourselves to fall into this trap. We can't be distracted when we work for money, and the more we make, the more we spend and the more we spend, the more we want. Ultimately, we know what comes out of this. If we are constantly chasing more and more and more, then money becomes an idol.

Jesus reminds us that all authority in heaven and on earth has been given to him. "For as many of you as were baptized into Christ have put on Christ. There is neither Jew nor Greek, there is neither slave nor free, there is no male and female, for you are all one in Christ Jesus. And if you are Christ's, then you are Abraham's offspring, heirs according to promise." (Matthew 28:17–20).

The context of this verse is leading to the Great Commission and how we are to go and make disciples, but while we don't want to take verses out of context, we also see this singular reality. All authority is given to him.

He is our boss. He is our leader in every way. He is in charge. That includes the fact that He is in charge of how we use our finances. And if we submit our finances to Jesus alone, we have to have wisdom in how we can use our money according to his character.

This means that the way we use our money can be an act of boldness. How can you be bold with your money?

Spend Your Money Wisely

The first step is simple and practical. Don't support groups that are anti-Christian.

If I wasn't willing to support BLM through a black square on social media, I'm certainly not going to support them financially. The same applies to any company or organization that is going to act in direct contradiction to Christianity.

The Bud Light boycott is another prime example here. They hired an influencer who lives a life contrary to Christian values. While many people made that political, it's also a moral and, ultimately, a scriptural issue.

God created us as man and woman. If a company is going to scoff at that and push an ideology outside of God's clear and appointed will, we can't support that company.

We have seen so many sexual- and gender-related boycotts over the past few years, including Planet Fitness and other gyms, sports franchises, Target, and more. Sometimes you can't help but spend your money at one of these companies, but if you have a choice, you should make the best choice you can. For example, I will usually not shop at Target due to their anti-Christian stance. Does that mean I never shop at Target? No. I have, and I will continue to do so when necessary, but it is rare that I need something only they have right away.

Another example is the airline industry. Unfortunately, almost all airlines have beliefs that are against Christianity. This means I have to choose the lesser of two evils if I want to fly. It's frustrating, but at times, I have little choice, and I simply have to do my best. And while some are trying to shift the industry, even banks have some anti-Christian beliefs so that it's nearly impossible to not have your money in a bank with values that contradict Scripture.

Make your stand and keep your money where it needs to be as

best you can. But speak out about why. Don't hesitate to say, "I don't shop at Target as their views don't align with mine." We don't have to organize a cancel campaign; Christianity is not a cancel culture. We just say no. We say, "I go somewhere else. My views are aligned with Christ, and their views are not. Therefore, they are at the bottom of my list when I want to buy something."

Belligerence would lead to cancel culture, but boldness leads to change.[71]

Get out of Debt

So many Americans and others in Western society are trapped in the area of debt. Debt is constantly available, Loans are a part of culture, and credit cards make up a significant portion of payment sources. It's no wonder that the average person in that culture has debt.

As of September 2024, the American government has well over thirty-five trillion dollars in debt. And if the nation's leaders can't decrease and pay off their debt, what example does that set for the people of the United States?

The average American household has $104,215 in debt,[72] which is fairly significant, given that the median household income in 2022 was $74,580,[73] according to the census bureau.

Views vary significantly on what debt is acceptable, how much debt is acceptable, or if debt is nothing more than theft. Dave Ramsey is a popular financial figure in the church world. He believes a fifteen-year mortgage is acceptable, but nothing else. Experts consider student debt to be good debt as it promotes future earnings potential.[74] YouTuber Caleb Hammer thinks there are "credit card

[71] Peter Demos, "Cancel culture is not civil disobedience, nor is it productive," March 1, 2024, *The Washington Times*, https://highergroundtimes.com/higherground/2024/mar/1/cancel-culture-is-not-civil-disobedience/.
[72] Jennifer Streaks, "Average American debt in 2024: Household debt statistics," July 31, 2024, *Business Insider*, https://www.businessinsider.com/personal-finance/credit-score/average-american-debt.
[73] Gloria Guzman and Melissa Kollar, " Income in the United States: 2022," September 12, 2023, Census.gov, https://www.census.gov/library/publications/2023/demo/p60-279.html.
[74] Kossondra Cloos, "Are Student Loans Worth it? What the Data Says," Earnest, March 25, 2025, https://www.earnest.com/blog/are-student-loans-worth-it/.

people" and "not credit card people," depending entirely upon the person's nature and self-discipline.[75]

Wherever you turn, you'll hear an opinion that you have to weigh as far as what it means for you and your situation. Is debt just a part of life that we have to learn to be comfortable with? Is it a necessary evil? Is debt inconvenient but ultimately unimportant when it comes to our faith? After all, what does debt have to do with boldness and the witness we carry?

Frankly, it's more important than we could ever give it credit for. The Bible addresses debt on a number of occasions. We've looked at the unforgiving servant who was forgiven debt and didn't forgive another, but that was in a completely different context.

As far as the lender and the debtor, the Bible is clear. "The rich rules over the poor, and the borrower is the slave of the lender" (Proverbs 22:7). Historically and in some parts of the world, literal enslavement results from loans and borrowing. In the US, we used to have debtors' prison for those who could not pay their debt. In our Western culture, we no longer do that or view debt as slavery, but debt still places people in bondage, nonetheless.

Even if you agree that a mortgage is acceptable debt, it doesn't change the fact that the actual translation of mortgage from the original French into English is "death pledge."[76] It holds us hostage to what we owe.

I never understood the true meaning of "the borrower is the slave of the lender" until my bank actually put me in this position. I bought a company that had a lot of debt, and when I decided to grow the business, I used debt as well. When I closed a store without telling the bank, they got mad. It did not impact my ability to make payments but actually enhanced it. I would have thought it was positive. After all, I was repaying them and had shown them the financials.

I met with the bank a few times, and they treated me terribly. They clearly didn't appreciate my strides to escape the grip of debt, but they wanted to control my business as they had such an investment in it. I didn't want to live that way anymore. As a result,

[75] Caleb Hammer, "Credit Card People," Caleb Hammer, October 8, 2024, https://calebhammer.com/credit-card-people/.
[76] *Merriam-Webster Dictionary*, "mortgage," accessed May 17, 2025, https://www.merriam-webster.com/dictionary/mortgage.

we are no longer with that bank. We currently have the lowest debt we have ever had.

In the business world, people fall into another line of thinking. Typically, the bank is forgiving when you have so much debt they can't afford to default on you. Businesses will rack up the debt, knowing they're now a liability if the bank holds them to the loans. This is unbiblical and is borderline theft. It's not like making shrewd, legal, and legitimate tax decisions. It's trickery.

But when a bank essentially owns you, you have to live by their rules. How can you speak up when they can control you? For example, what if your boss is asking you to do something evil or against God's Word? Can you risk missing the mortgage payment? Can you risk missing the next credit card payment? If you have outstanding debts, you don't have an option to miss work or, worse, lose your job, and it's a miserable place to be in. You have to decide between feeding your family and keeping the roof over your head if you don't have an income.

Like so many of the examples we have looked at, there is a risk. Recently, a teacher in Ireland lost his job because he was unwilling to support gender ideology in the classroom due to his Christian faith. Except they weren't content to just take away his job. This was the third time he has spent a stint in prison since his initial jail time in 2022 for refusing to use a student's preferred pronouns. The next two occasions landed him in jail because he refused to follow a court order to stay away from the school. He believes he has a right to go and teach, despite disagreeing with school policies.[77] He has also faced financial penalties beyond just losing his job and being imprisoned.

Each of us has to honestly ask ourselves if we could stand so boldly and lose so much in our current financial state. Do we have the savings we need? Or are we bound by debt with such high monthly expenses that we couldn't make it more than a few days without a paycheck?

Getting out of debt paves the way for us to be bolder. We don't

---

[77] Ray Lewis, "Irish teacher jailed for third time over pronouns dispute: 'disgrace on our country,'" WPFO, September 4, 2024, https://fox23maine.com/news/nation-world/irish-teacher-jailed-for-third-time-over-pronouns-dispute-disgrace-on-our-country-enoch-burke-wilsons-hospital-school-ireland-preferred-pronouns-lgbt-transgender-gender-identity.

have to have a fortune to fall back on, but we should at least work toward freedom from owing others.

Furthermore, in a country that encourages debt, consumerism, and keeping up with Joneses, getting out of debt is a bold move. It tells people your priorities are not found in the things of the world but in the things of God. It becomes clear we are seeking something greater and more valuable than what our debt can buy us in the meantime.

As usual, however, we can't just get out of debt and suddenly be considered bold. We have to tell people *why* we chose this lifestyle. We have to tell people we are choosing to be wise with our finances because we don't want to be beholden to anyone but Jesus. We want it to be clear: He is the only master we want to serve. He has already paid our debts, and we seek to live according to his will because he is the way, the truth, and the life.

Truly, debt is an obstacle that must be addressed to allow you to be bolder.

A Trap to Avoid

One final note on using our finances for the sake of boldness is to remember how to respond when we see others who have so much despite being terrible people. Yes, your enemies may have more than you. They may have mansions, private jets, and one-hundred-thousand-dollar bodies. Or their house may be just a little bigger than yours, shoes just a little nicer, and a car that's a bit newer. It doesn't matter.

When we look at people who are not living biblically, we can become bitter when we see how well they're doing. It can hurt us a little to think they are being rewarded despite doing nothing to serve God. We can get frustrated when we realize we want what they have. Don't feel that way. Their temporary luxury is nothing compared to your eternity. They may have some amazing possessions in this world, but those won't last.

What God has in store for you is greater than anything they could dream of. It would be nice if we could prosper here on earth, and many believers in Christ do have a lot of money, but that is not where eternity is found, and we have to be okay with that.

In the book of Psalms, Asaph spoke to this. He understood. But he also knew where his true hope was found.

Truly God is good to Israel,
    to those who are pure in heart.
But as for me, my feet had almost stumbled,
    my steps had nearly slipped.
For I was envious of the arrogant
when I saw the prosperity of the wicked. . . .
Behold, these are the wicked;
    always at ease, they increase in riches. . . .
For behold, those who are far from you shall perish;
    you put an end to everyone who is unfaithful to you.
But for me it is good to be near God;
    I have made the Lord God my refuge,
That I may tell of all your works.
(Psalm 73:1–3, 12, 27–28)

For Reflection

1. Consider how viewing money as a gift from God shifts your perspective on wealth. How does this perspective influence your attitude toward spending, saving, and giving?

2. What are some ways that money can be a blessing but also a potential curse as mentioned in the chapter? How can you use money wisely to glorify God and avoid the negative effects of materialism?

3. How do you personally balance the pursuit of financial security with trusting God for your needs? What steps can you take to ensure that money doesn't become an idol or source of anxiety?

4. In your own life, how can spending money wisely be a form of standing against culture? What organizations or causes do you avoid supporting because of your faith?

5. Consider how tithing strengthens your faith in God's provision. How does giving sacrificially, even when money is tight, help you trust in God to meet your needs?

6. How does being in debt affect your ability to live boldly for Christ? How might becoming debt-free help you better serve God and others with greater flexibility and generosity?

7. What does Proverbs 22:7 teach us about the dangers of debt? How does this principle apply to our modern consumer-driven culture? How does this apply to our consumer-driven culture, and what steps can you take to avoid falling into financial bondage?

8. Reflect on how societal pressures to conform to materialistic standards can lead to poor financial decisions. How can you approach your financial responsibilities with wisdom and discernment, avoiding the temptation to keep up with the Joneses?

CHAPTER TWENTY-TWO

Speak Out Loud in the Platforms God Gave You

This is probably the chapter most people expected when they picked up this book—and what led others not to pick up this book. This is the boldness that requires us to step forward in our faith by standing firm in the truth.

God has given everyone platforms in which to use their voices. Work, family, extended family, book club, social media, or any other number of arenas can be used to step out in faith and speak up. Our platforms are all around us. Start in these platforms. You do not need to go far or look for stadiums for opportunities to be bold. Start where you're at. Even in areas where you may not have an ongoing relationship, you should start.

I shared my story about my interaction at Whole Foods and the conversation that arose. Times like this are a perfect opportunity to speak up and just dialogue. You may not answer every last question a person has, and they may not turn to God in that moment, but your boldness will at least open a door and give you a chance to share the gospel so that person starts thinking about your conversation.

People are drawn to humble, respectful boldness. They appreciate challenging conversations as long as the other side shows them dignity. You can be honest and bold, sharing the truth of Jesus with love, anywhere the door is open.

Where you are anxious or worried, lean into Christ for strength. Remember the common pitfalls we discussed and go back through the questions at the end of each chapter. How can you arm yourself against those pitfalls? How can you make sure they don't stop you from doing what God has called you to do?

Whether you are with friends or getting groceries, you will be met with opportunities to share the truth. Don't miss them. Use the moment when it's handed to you.

Acts 8 includes several stories of men preaching the gospel. We first see Philip proclaiming Christ in Samaria, which led to multiple healings.

> Now those who were scattered went about preaching the word. Philip went down to the city of Samaria and proclaimed to them the Christ. And the crowds with one accord paid attention to what was being said by Philip, when they heard him and saw the signs that he did. For unclean spirits, crying out with a loud voice, came out of many who had them, and many who were paralyzed or lame were healed. So there was much joy in that city. (Acts 8:4–8)

Simon the Magician believes but is then denounced when he wants the power of healing through his former magician practices. He begs for mercy as a result.

From there, we see Philip meeting the Ethiopian Eunuch. After some discussion of Scripture, the conversation follows.

> And the eunuch said to Philip, "About whom, I ask you, does the prophet say this, about himself or about someone else?" Then Philip opened his mouth, and beginning with this Scripture he told him the good news about Jesus. And as they were going along the road they came to some water, and the eunuch said, "See, here is water! What prevents me from being baptized?" And he commanded the chariot to stop, and they both went down into the water, Philip and the eunuch, and he baptized him. And when they came up out of the water, the Spirit of the Lord carried Philip away, and the eunuch saw him no more, and went on his way rejoicing.

But Philip found himself at Azotus, and as he passed through he preached the gospel to all the towns until he came to Caesarea. (Acts 8:34–40)

Throughout the book of Acts, in many places, the early church establishes itself through bold yet simple encounters. The apostles would stand and preach the gospel in the markets where they worked, in the synagogues, on the road as they traveled, in prison, with the wealthy or poor, with neighbors and with strangers. It didn't matter with whom they came into contact. They preached the gospel.

Their platform was wherever their feet took them. We should view our life the same way. While we aren't establishing the early church the way these men were, it is still our duty to live boldly and declare our faith without fear. We should always live with the confidence that an opportunity to share the gospel is the most important opportunity we have.

Maybe you work in ministry and it is actually your job to preach or maybe you are a stay-at-home-mom discipling your children and occasionally interacting with other moms at the park and you share your faith that way. Whatever your calling, sharing the gospel is part of it.

An Unexpected Encounter

Art Thomas tells a story about a time God spoke to him. One day, he was at Sam's Club getting his groceries, and he felt the Holy Spirit say that he needed to pray for healing for the cashier's neck. He didn't want to because it would be uncomfortable to even ask about her neck. He was in a public place and didn't know her. She hadn't spoken to him or asked for anything.

Art kept trying to say no to God, but God kept pushing him, so he finally stepped out of his comfort zone and relented. He had to acknowledge to her that it was weird for him, and he wasn't going to touch her. Once she agreed, Art said something like, "Neck, be healed in Jesus's name." The woman's neck was healed instantly.

These circumstances don't always happen, but sometimes they do. Sometimes Jesus calls us out of our comfort zone even when we don't know why. The Holy Spirit moves us to take a bold and uncomfortable step of faith.

In this instance, Art could have continued to refuse. He could have ignored the Holy Spirit calling him to pray for this woman's healing. But ultimately, that would have left her with neck problems and him with guilt for ignoring God's leading on his heart.

I've shared already about encounters when I didn't respond when I could have and times when I thought about it later, regretting that I hadn't first thought to share the gospel. But when we do feel the leading of the Holy Spirit, we have to be prepared to speak. We have to understand it is a gift to be able to share the truth with others, even when it may not be convenient or comfortable.

You may be thinking, *That sounds great, Peter, but how am I supposed to do a 180 like that? Now I'm scared to go to the grocery store or to work, in case I suddenly have to stand in front of everyone and preach.*

Boldness is not always inherent in our being. It takes time, training, and wisdom. You do have to make the choice to start, of course. You can't put it off forever and expect that boldness will just come when the time is right.

Like most skills, you first have to practice. Practice with believers if that makes you more comfortable. Practice hearing your voice as you share the gospel or try to answer the difficult questions. You can even go through a list of challenging biblical questions online and answer them out loud while you're sitting alone just to get comfortable with the responses.

You can read through the Heidelberg or Westminster catechisms to learn the questions and answers to understand some of the theological foundations of Christianity. Or you can watch YouTube videos where progressives try to challenge believers and, before you listen to the response of the Christian featured, pause the video and answer in your own words.

We can practice our responses in so many ways even though we have no idea what people will actually say to challenge us in the moment. Knowing what you would say to arguments that could be adjacent to those thrust at you is just as helpful in defending your faith.

The Bible reminds us of the importance of preparing and knowing the foundations of our faith. If we are rooted in truth, we can answer anything. We may not have the perfect response—we may need to tell the other person we will dig deeper and then get back to them. But if we are rooted in truth, we can hold to Christ as the cornerstone and give an accurate and honest answer based on our understanding of Scripture and who God is. We must prepare to make a defense.

> Now who is there to harm you if you are zealous for what is good? But even if you should suffer for righteousness' sake, you will be blessed. Have no fear of them, nor be troubled, but in your hearts honor Christ the Lord as holy, always being prepared to make a defense to anyone who asks you for a reason for the hope that is in you; yet do it with gentleness and respect, having a good conscience, so that, when you are slandered, those who revile your good behavior in Christ may be put to shame. For it is better to suffer for doing good, if that should be God's will, than for doing evil. (1 Peter 3:13–17)

One of our problems is that we forget what we are going to say in the moment. It's easy to get flustered or nervous when we are suddenly put in a situation where we do actually have to speak up. If we aren't prepared ahead of time, we might mentally shut down. And like I said, we can't realistically prepare ahead to answer every single little question. But the more you practice and say what you do expect, the more confidence you gain, and you can get better at it.

Remember when you had to memorize a poem for school back in the day? You started with the first several lines, and then you added to it, little by little, and kept adding to it until you memorized all of it.

And you don't have to wait for the perfect opportunity. To begin with, practice in safe areas where you are more comfortable. For instance, I like telemarketing people. I can practice with them, and they hang up. No harm. The best-case scenario is that they want to know more about Jesus. The worst-case scenario is they hang up, and I don't have to deal with them. It just depends on whether or not God moves in their spirit at that moment.

I can practice with a grocery store clerk, and if it doesn't go well, I will probably never have to see them again. I am extra bold when I travel. While traveling, I can share the gospel and gain practice but without ever facing them again if it goes poorly. I can leave that encounter and pray that God would send someone else to them—someone who can communicate more effectively with them. But no matter what, I speak out when I get the chance.

Don't be the person that timidly hands someone a pamphlet and walks away. I was at a gas station pumping gas, and a lady behind me meekly said, "Excuse me." I turned to a middle-aged woman dressed very conservatively, and she handed me a pamphlet from the Jehovah's Witnesses and walked away before I even saw what it was. By the time I recognized it, she was in her car driving off.

Many Christians see Jehovah's witnesses as a cult, which makes our imitation of their strategies uniquely worse. But they use similar methods. We see it at the restaurant all the time. They won't talk with anyone about their faith or hope, and then they leave a Christian pamphlet behind with the tip.

That is not bold. It makes Christians look weak because they have to rely on a piece of paper to communicate and they aren't willing to share themselves. It shows we don't know how to respond if someone challenges us.

Truly, we have to get used to hearing the sound of our voice. The late David Pawson recommended that when we pray at home, we should pray out loud so we can get used to hearing our voice as we talk to God.[78] The same is true of your testimony and, certainly, when we speak up about clearly wrong beliefs, words, or behaviors. We need to hear ourselves speak about these topics aloud so we can grow comfortable when the time comes to actually share them with others.

I can assure you that you will grow in confidence, but you will go through stages of being uncomfortable. It's just like working out—you must develop your muscles, and they will stretch. It's uncomfortable. Like with education, you have to challenge your brain, and you will be uncomfortable. Spiritual discipline and boldness are no different. If we do not exercise and go through uncomfortable seasons, then we will lose strength in these areas as well.

Think about where you need to start. Look at concentric circles, e.g., a dartboard. You are the center. Start by talking openly to those in the next circle. When you get comfortable, then move to the next circle. Keep moving outward as God leads you, and you can continue to grow in confidence and strength. (On the other hand, as I mentioned earlier, sometimes it might be easier to talk to someone

---

[78] David Pawson, *Practising the Principles of Prayer* (True Potential, 2008).

in the outermost circle, the person you will never see again.)

Each time you move to the next circle, it becomes more uncomfortable. Don't expect a visible result. You have no idea what fruit the Holy Spirit will produce when you speak to even one person. You may never see the end result or know the impact of a single conversation, but that doesn't matter. We don't share the gospel so we can tally up the salvations that resulted from our conversations. We share the gospel because we long for others to know about this incredible gift. We have to learn to love others more than we fear them. We have to be more passionate about the salvation of others than we are frightened by their response.

A Chain Reaction of Faith

D.L. Moody started out as a shoe salesman. Someone was working beside him; some reports say it was his boss, Edward Kimble. Kimble shared the gospel with him, and as a result, D.L. became one of the most effective evangelists in the 1800s. D.L. won thousands upon thousands of people to Christ, many of whom, in turn, did something similar.[79]

One of the people who heard Moody preach and who responded to the gospel was Frederick Meyer. Ultimately, he, too, went nationwide, preaching the gospel. Wilbur Chapman heard him and converted and started a ministry with an ex-baseball player who was also converted by a street evangelist and was named Billy Sunday.[80] Billy Sunday, an amazing evangelist in his own right, preached in Charlotte, NC. He was so well-liked that they invited him back. However, Billy Sunday couldn't attend, so he recommended Mordecai Ham, who drew some protests.

One young boy was asked to come to the meetings but didn't want to. When he heard of the protests, he decided he wanted to see what the commotion was all about. There, he was converted. That young boy was Billy Graham, who led many revivals in the United States and worldwide; his preaching has reached millions of people

---

[79] Jean Priestap, "It Started With a Sunday School Teacher!," Vision for Christ, March 8, 2017, https://visionforchristworld.com/it-started-with-a-sunday-school-teacher/.
[80] Ibid.

and his fruit keeps growing.[81]

Here is a summary of the influence of these men. DL Moody won Billy Sunday to Jesus. From the witness of Billy Sunday, Billy Graham became a Christian. Billy Graham preached to millions worldwide, with many people giving their lives to Christ at his conferences. For those who did genuinely become Christ followers as a result of the Billy Graham crusades, their faith can be traced back to a shoe salesman. Who shared the gospel with Edward Kimble? And who shared the gospel with the person who shared the gospel with Kimble?

We can see what a magnificent chain reaction happened when someone is bold enough to share their faith. It all started with one person telling his coworker about the love of Christ. He had no idea the impact it would have, but it didn't stop him.

The Faithful Vet

George and Betty Jackson, the founders of my local church, had a wonderful story as well. George was a vet who originally worked on horses. He was fairly well-known in his practice in the area. Betty, his wife, was pregnant with her third child, but they found she had cancer and was going to die. George and Betty went to church but weren't very strong believers. Their attendance was more cultural than based on a deep belief.

On a plane to the Mayo Clinic for an appointment with the oncologist, Betty prayed that God would reveal the truth to her before she died. She wanted to teach her children the true religion (Baptist, Methodist, Presbyterian, etc.). Something in her recognized she needed to know the truth and not just live a moral life. She wanted to make sure she left a legacy to her children that would set them up with the assurance of faith.

But when she arrived at the clinic, the cancer was completely gone. It had completely vanished from her body. George and Betty were later mentored by Derek Prince, and as a result, they met the Holy Spirit. He used his vet practice to talk about Jesus and ultimately led a Bible study. Eventually, that turned into a church with a tent. Although their church was based in a small country town in Tennessee, George and Betty called it World Outreach Church.

---

[81] Ibid.

Their son, now the lead pastor, still laughs at the thought of naming a church in a tent "World Outreach," but now they have significant ministries spreading to the world, including Russia and Israel, with a very large national TV and internet presence. Their church is well-known and well-attended. The outreach has continued to grow.

As of this writing, Betty died a few weeks ago. When she died, all the people in the visitation line shared about the impact she had on them. They were there for hours, telling their stories. Her influence was huge because she told people about Jesus, and her boldness spread to generations to come. I got to speak with her face-to-face a dozen times or so, and it was unreal. She was a very short woman with so much peace from knowing the Holy Spirit.

Everything that has come from our church started simply from them having conversations at the vet clinic and asking people about their story. George and Betty just talked to the people who brought their animals. But it became a great, wonderful movement within the community and the church as a whole.

Too often, we don't think we have much impact, but God uses our stories. He uses us in ways that transition from our humble words and subpar attempts to share the gospel into dramatic and wonderful change for others in the world.

The words of Jesus explain it better than anyone else could.

That same day Jesus went out of the house and sat beside the sea. And great crowds gathered about him, so that he got into a boat and sat down. And the whole crowd stood on the beach. And he told them many things in parables, saying: "A sower went out to sow. And as he sowed, some seeds fell along the path, and the birds came and devoured them. Other seeds fell on rocky ground, where they did not have much soil, and immediately they sprang up, since they had no depth of soil, but when the sun rose they were scorched. And since they had no root, they withered away. Other seeds fell among thorns, and the thorns grew up and choked them. Other seeds fell on good soil and produced grain, some a hundredfold, some sixty, some thirty. He who has ears, let him hear. (Matthew 13:1–9)

From there, Jesus gives an explanation.

Hear then the parable of the sower: When anyone hears the word of the kingdom and does not understand it, the evil one comes and snatches away what has been sown in his heart. This is what was sown along the path. As for what was sown on rocky ground, this is the one who hears the word and immediately receives it with joy, yet he has no root in himself, but endures for a while, and when tribulation or persecution arises on account of the word, immediately he falls away. As for what was sown among thorns, this is the one who hears the word, but the cares of the world and the deceitfulness of riches choke the word, and it proves unfruitful. As for what was sown on good soil, this is the one who hears the word and understands it. He indeed bears fruit and yields, in one case a hundredfold, in another sixty, and in another thirty. (Matthew 13:18–23)

If the sower does his duty to sow seeds where they should be sown, the end result is fruit that yields fruit that yields fruit.

One tomato seed will sprout one tomato plant. But that tomato plant could produce a hundred tomatoes, depending on the variety. Each of those hundred tomatoes contains a hundred seeds. Each of those seeds can be planted. And each subsequent plant will only produce more.

It's remarkable what can come of a seed. If God has called us to plant them, we must obey and do just that. We never know if we are the gardener or just the one who plants the seed. God might intend for someone else to water and nurture those seeds each day. He determines that and uses the Holy Spirit to do so. But no amount of water, compost, or fertilizer will grow a seed that was never planted.

Our calling and greatest joy and gift is to share the gospel and see lives changed. Who knows if the person will respond or not? They may ignore you and live their life in sinful doubt. Or they may become a world-changer who shares the gospel will millions.

We think that if we're not a Billy Graham, it doesn't matter whether or not we use our platform. But we can powerfully impact others to make monumental changes just by standing boldly when called upon to do so. And to this, we are called.

For Reflection

1. What does boldness in faith mean to you, and how does it apply to your daily life? How have you been bold in your faith in the past, and how can you cultivate more boldness in your daily interactions, both big and small?

2. Consider the different "platforms" in your life—work, family, community, social media, etc. How can you use these to share your faith and speak boldly for Christ?

3. Reflect on your immediate social circle—family, friends, coworkers. What small steps can you take to be more open about your faith with them and to step out in boldness?

4. Reflect on the fears or anxieties you feel when sharing your faith. Are they rooted in personal insecurity, fear of rejection, concern about conflict, or something else? How can you overcome these challenges and step forward in boldness?

5. Why is it important to start where you're at when it comes to speaking the truth of the gospel, and how does this influence your approach to boldness?

6. How can we prepare ourselves to share the gospel, even when we don't know the exact questions we will face? How can you grow in confidence, knowing that God will provide the words and the wisdom when the time comes?

7. Consider how practicing boldness in low-risk environments (family, friends, small groups) can help you build confidence before stepping into more challenging situations. What are some practical ways to start?

8. Think about what it would look like to make boldness a daily habit, not just a singular moment of action. How can you consistently practice boldness in your everyday life?

9. Reflect on how sharing the gospel is an act of faith, even if

you never see the immediate results. How can you trust God with the outcome, knowing that the act itself is a success?

CHAPTER TWENTY-THREE

Consequences of Being

or Not Being Bold

At some point in your life as a believer in Christ, you have to make a choice. Will you be bold or not? Either choice comes with consequences. You have to choose which option fits best with what matters to you personally.

Are you ready to lose the things of this world by being bold? Can you call yourself a believer if you don't entirely give your life over to God? It's up to you.

To Not Be Bold

Sometimes we are not bold by choice. Other times, it is by mistake. I shared a few of my stories: times I was bold, times I wasn't, and times I missed opportunities because my thoughts were elsewhere. I think back to that morning walk in Vegas when my instincts led me to flee like Joseph fleeing from Potiphar's wife when I ought to have recognized God giving me an opportunity to share the gospel with a broken woman.

In times like these, you do have a choice. Maybe you leave and realize you missed the opportunity. You can then make the decision to pay closer attention in the future. You don't want to miss those chances again. I had to start praying for open eyes to see clearly when God was giving me a chance to reach out to someone. I didn't want to miss another chance to present the gospel.

If you find yourself frequently in situations when you think back on missed opportunities, recognize the pattern. Take time to pray that God will open your eyes when you are in the moment. Ask him to help you see before it's too late so you aren't left regretting a lost opportunity later and wishing you had handled the situation differently.

Practice self-awareness and keeping your eyes open. Your situation may not change right away, but you will start to see these opportunities more readily and not miss them as often.

At times, we take too long to build up the courage to speak up. I've struggled with this as well. Sometimes we know the Holy Spirit is leading us to step out in faith, but we need to psych ourselves up before we're ready. We need to quickly pray for boldness, ask God for help, or even ask him for a sign. We hesitate, take a deep breath, and think, *Are you sure you want me to do that?* We hope he will say no, but most of the time, we can't deny or ignore the reality that he is prompting us to speak. We have to actually follow through, right?

But at times, we wait so long that sometimes we miss the opportunity altogether. The moment passes. The person leaves. We didn't even see them leaving, or we certainly would have followed them out—right? Surely God didn't *actually* mean for us to go to them or he would have made it happen. We come up with the excuses, but really we just missed our chance when it was right in front of us. We could have obeyed and done exactly what God was asking, but we were too weak and afraid of the response, so we delayed. Ultimately, we have to pray God will send a bold person to reach out to that person since we failed to do so.

That's an important point. Whether or not you choose to be bold, you will fail. That's okay. As we already said, boldness requires practice. It doesn't come easily or right away. Some days, it's hard. Some days, we just don't know what to say or do. We may struggle just to smile at a person, let alone share the eternal, glorious truth of eternal life with them.

Our God is just and righteous, demanding that we, too, be just, righteous, and holy. But he knows we can't be that. We need his strength. We have to lean on the completed work of Christ on the cross, who was resurrected for our redemption. Only he can take failures like us and create victorious disciples who freely share the gospel.

Did you want to fail in that moment? Did you want to give up or be weak? Did you want to see that person leave without hearing the gospel? Of course not. But this is a journey, and we have to fight our instincts and do better next time. We engage in a works mindset, not because we are so strong that our actions can contribute to our obedience and salvation. We do it because God has been so gracious and merciful as to save us and give us his strength to improve and grow deeper and be bolder.

At times, we simply choose not to be bold. It's too uncomfortable. It's too awkward. It's too inconvenient. Or, oftentimes, it's too likely to cause division between us and someone else.

Do we want to make this choice regularly? No. But it is in our nature. We don't want to experience those negative things, so we may choose to avoid boldness more often than not. We may give up and not practice what we say we value.

If that's the case, it's time to repent. We can't keep making excuses and pretending we will do better next time when, in reality, next time is going to be just as difficult, and we probably won't make a different choice.

If we choose not to be bold, we need to analyze why. What is at the root of it? How can we work on that and do better? How can we make a change in our own lives and in the lives of others? We have to hold ourselves accountable and not just slip into the comfortable rhythm that tells us it's okay to be weak. Accepting our failures is not the same thing as dwelling in them and making excuses.

We can choose not to be bold because we simply don't ever want to be bold. We've read through the common underlying reasons for lacking boldness, and ultimately, it's a nice thought to change, but how can we? For some people, it's just not worth the change of heart, mind, and soul. We can profess with our mouths that Jesus is Lord, but are we truly willing to take on the potential consequences of speaking out when necessary?

The Bible plainly gives us our choice, really just two choices: to obey or not to obey. As we saw earlier in this book, boldness is a command. It's not just a nice idea or something we should strive for. It's a matter of obedience. So when God lays out the clear options, we have to recognize exactly what that means for us. Which consequence will we choose?

> See, I am setting before you today a blessing and a curse: the blessing, if you obey the commandments of the Lord your God, which I command you today, and the curse, if you do not obey the commandments of the Lord your God, but turn aside from the way that I am commanding you today, to go after other gods that you have not known. (Deuteronomy 11:26–28)

Why take the chance? Why give up eternity for temporary satisfaction today? We are so uncomfortable in our lives on earth. But why do we believe it deserves more of our attention than the beauty of heaven? Do we want to chase the gods of this world instead of living obediently for the God who created all things?

The Bible says that if we deny Christ here, he will deny us in eternity.

> So everyone who acknowledges me before men, I also will acknowledge before my Father who is in heaven, but whoever denies me before men, I also will deny before my Father who is in heaven.
>
> Do not think that I have come to bring peace to the earth. I have not come to bring peace, but a sword. For I have come to set a man against his father, and a daughter against her mother, and a daughter-in-law against her mother-in-law. And a person's enemies will be those of his own household. Whoever loves father or mother more than me is not worthy of me, and whoever loves son or daughter more than me is not worthy of me. And whoever does not take his cross and follow me is not worthy of me. Whoever finds his life will lose it, and whoever loses his life for my sake will find it.
>
> Whoever receives you receives me, and whoever receives me receives him who sent me. The one who receives a prophet because he is a prophet will receive a prophet's reward, and the one who receives a righteous

person because he is a righteous person will receive a righteous person's reward. And whoever gives one of these little ones even a cup of cold water because he is a disciple, truly, I say to you, he will by no means lose his reward. (Matthew 10:32–42)

The Bible also tells us cowards go into the lake of fire. After all, if we are not living obediently, we are cursed, we will lose our eternal life and our righteous reward, and our names will not be found in the book of life.

Then I saw a great white throne and him who was seated on it. From his presence earth and sky fled away, and no place was found for them. And I saw the dead, great and small, standing before the throne, and books were opened. Then another book was opened, which is the book of life. And the dead were judged by what was written in the books, according to what they had done. And the sea gave up the dead who were in it, Death and Hades gave up the dead who were in them, and they were judged, each one of them, according to what they had done. Then Death and Hades were thrown into the lake of fire. This is the second death, the lake of fire. And if anyone's name was not found written in the book of life, he was thrown into the lake of fire. (Revelation 20:11–15)

Stacking these portions of Scripture shows us exactly what the consequences are if we choose to avoid boldness. We need to consider our place in one hundred years and not next week. Where will you be in eternity? Is it worth it just to stay comfortable for a couple of more years?

If you're reading this book, I expect you are seeking a way to be bold. I hope you aren't content to settle for pulling back. But again, you will have times of failure and a season of learning. If you really don't want to go down the path of the coward, pray relentlessly that God will forgive the weakness of the past and lead you into a place where you are unashamed of the truth and passionately seeking to stand.

To Be Bold

You can lose freedom, family, friends, and even your life by standing up when it's hard to do so. Nevertheless, if we are making the choice to be bold, we know it's worth it. We know Christ is worth it. We know the disciples lost their lives because it was worth it.

If we are going to lose the things of this world, we need to lose them for something we truly believe in, something truly worth our lives. What is more important than the God of creation and the merciful Son who have given us eternity? What is more important than the Holy Spirit that walks beside us and leads us through the good and the bad each day? Is there anything more worth our lives than living for the truth?

We know persecution will come. The Bible is clear that in the last days, persecution will be rampant and believers will suffer. Whatever you believe about the last days, whether they happen any time after the resurrection or during the last few decades before he returns or as a seven-year trial, we know persecution will probably only get worse.

However, we also know many places around the world have experienced much persecution long before now. In the United States, we can easily get caught up thinking we are in the end times because morality is slipping rapidly away from culture. But how long have Chinese Christians experienced persecution? How long did the Ethiopian Church have to go underground before a political change allowed them to publicly practice their beliefs again? How many Christians were fed to lions in Rome?

Persecution ebbs and flows. While it seems to be getting worse and darkness is spreading, we are not God, and we don't know what he has planned next. What we do know is that no matter how dark it gets, he is the light of the world. As America and other Western societies seem to be stripping away the rights of Christians, one day at a time, we can rest in the peace of knowing God is still faithful and that we can and must endure persecution.

> Behold, I am sending you out as sheep in the midst of wolves, so be wise as serpents and innocent as doves. Beware of men, for they will deliver you over to courts and flog you in their synagogues, and you will be dragged before

governors and kings for my sake, to bear witness before them and the Gentiles. When they deliver you over, do not be anxious how you are to speak or what you are to say, for what you are to say will be given to you in that hour. For it is not you who speak, but the Spirit of your Father speaking through you. Brother will deliver brother over to death, and the father his child, and children will rise against parents and have them put to death, and you will be hated by all for my name's sake. But the one who endures to the end will be saved. When they persecute you in one town, flee to the next, for truly, I say to you, you will not have gone through all the towns of Israel before the Son of Man comes. (Matthew 10:16–23)

Whatever our current hour, we must choose boldness. Whatever the cost, we must choose boldness. The cost of cowardice is far greater.

Self-denial for the sake of boldness is a part of being a Christian. We can use all the excuses we want. We can fall for the world's lies and say it's unloving to hurt someone's feelings by pushing the truth on them. We can say we have to bend to certain rules because we can't risk losing our job since God has called us to feed and provide for our families. We can twist and shape matters in a way that makes our lives easier.

But if we are not conforming our hearts to the truth and standing up for it, we aren't living as Christians. If we, on the other hand, choose to submit to the will of the Lord and be bold, we are demonstrating what really matters.

Our souls are at stake. Not just our jobs, not just our relationships, and not just our lives. It is eternity. And choosing boldness, though difficult and full of all kinds of earthly troubles, is the worthy endeavor.

Then Jesus told his disciples, "If anyone would come after me, let him deny himself and take up his cross and follow me. For whoever would save his life will lose it, but whoever loses his life for my sake will find it. For what will it profit a man if he gains the whole world and forfeits his soul? Or what shall a man give in return for his soul?" (Matthew 16:24–26)

Will we lose what we love in this life? Or will we lose eternity? It's time to decide.

For Reflection

1. Think about times when you've missed opportunities to share your faith or stand up for what you believe in. What are the common barriers that prevent you from acting in boldness?

2. Have you ever regretted not taking the opportunity to share the gospel or stand up for what you believe in? How did that regret affect you spiritually? What can you learn from those moments to make bolder choices in the future?

3. Why do you think some Christians choose not to be bold in sharing their faith? Is it fear, insecurity, or something else? How can self-examination help uncover the root causes of our reluctance to be bold?

4. What do you think the cost of boldness might look like for you? Are there relationships, comforts, or opportunities you may need to sacrifice in order to be bold for Christ? How does Christ's call to take up our cross inform your response?

5. The call to deny oneself and take up one's cross is central to the Christian life. What does self-denial look like in practice when it comes to living out boldness for Christ?

6. Reflecting on Matthew 10:32–42, how does the promise of eternal reward (even in the face of suffering) shape your understanding of the importance of boldness in the Christian walk? How does this hope shape your approach to living with boldness today?

CHAPTER TWENTY-FOUR

It's So Worth It

What does the Bible say about heaven? Why do our hearts so badly long to be there? Why are we striving to spend eternity there?

People have a number of different focuses when talking about heaven. Some can't wait to see their loved ones who have passed away. Some think of how beautiful it must be, with crowns, mansions, and streets of gold. But will heaven be a party where we leave our mansion that morning, straighten our crown, and prance down the street to Grandma's house? Probably not.

I really do not know what it will be like, but I do know this. There will be a new heaven. There will be a new earth. We will rule and get our rewards from our works here. There will be no more sorrow. No loneliness. No hate. No sin. But why?

Because God dwells there.

Eternity is worth the sacrifice of our comfort, convenience, and confidence. It is worth everything to stand before the throne of God above and be told, "Well done, good and faithful servant" (Matthew 25:21).

The Mercy of Heaven

> Then I saw a new heaven and a new earth, for the first heaven and the first earth had passed away, and the sea was no more. And I saw the holy city, new Jerusalem, coming down out of heaven from God, prepared as a bride adorned for her husband. And I heard a loud voice from the throne saying, "Behold, the dwelling place of God is with man. He will dwell with them, and they will be his people, and God himself will be with them as their God. He will wipe away every tear from their eyes, and death shall be no more, neither shall there be mourning, nor crying, nor pain anymore, for the former things have passed away." (Revelation 21:1–4)

Heaven is a place of mercy, a place of refuge. When this temporary earth passes away in one form or another, we will be in a perfect, beautiful place God has prepared for us.

These verses show us the image of God wiping away our tears. What greater image of a loving Father can we hope for than one who stands before us and wipes the tears from our eyes? No matter the pain we experience in this world, from financial strain to depression to facing execution for our faith, he will take those tears from us.

Heaven is a merciful place where there is no more death. We have eternal life, always. There is no more mourning, crying, or pain. These are the promises we have in heaven. The former things will pass away, including our weaknesses and our cowardice. The lack of confidence and comfort that bind us here and prevent us from being bold will pass away. They mean nothing in eternity. And if we are in Christ, that means they mean nothing to us now.

In the last chapter, we covered that realistically, we will fail. We will fall into our sin nature in this world, and we will have moments where we don't know how to be bold. But if we have the mindset of our identity in Christ, it gets easier to recognize that temporary insecurities are pointless to dwell on.

Changing our perspective from living in a cruel, fallen world to striving for the mercies of heaven allows us to recognize what matters most and to do the right thing.

The Restoration of Heaven

> At the end of the days I, Nebuchadnezzar, lifted my eyes to heaven, and my reason returned to me, and I blessed the Most High, and praised and honored him who lives forever,
>
> for his dominion is an everlasting dominion,
>   and his kingdom endures from generation to generation;
> all the inhabitants of the earth are accounted as nothing,
>   and he does according to his will among the host of heaven
>   and among the inhabitants of the earth;
>   and none can stay his hand
>   or say to him, "What have you done?"
>
> At the same time my reason returned to me, and for the glory of my kingdom, my majesty and splendor returned to me. My counselors and my lords sought me, and I was established in my kingdom, and still more greatness was added to me. Now I, Nebuchadnezzar, praise and extol and honor the King of heaven, for all his works are right and his ways are just; and those who walk in pride he is able to humble. (Daniel 4:34–37)

This passage from Daniel shows us another side of heaven. King Nebuchadnezzar was a mess. He had become like an animal (not so different from what culture encourages these days, after all). In the midst of his madness and the chaos he had allowed in his heart, God showed him mercy. This mercy led to Nebuchadnezzar's restoration. He looked up to heaven and saw the mercy of redemption. He began to praise God and let go of his pride.

Heaven is a place of restoration because it is the dwelling place of the God who restores. Even a man of great pride is humbled because he sees the glory of God and knows that only God can do such magnificent works.

When we see this restoration, it's easy to long for it. Living in a world that is broken, we desire wonder. When we are amidst chaos, we desire order. In heaven is perfect order and wonder with a perfect balance of grace and truth.

Living in the mercy of heaven frees us from the pain of a broken world. The restoration of heaven frees us from our broken selves.

In his mercy, God meets us in our pain, but in restoration, we are so in awe of his glory and magnificence that it's impossible to look at ourselves. If we are living with too much introspection, we may find ourselves overwhelmed with despair. We need to be self-aware, but introspection can lead to despair and self-centeredness. Looking instead to heaven and to the glory of God brings hope and life to our hearts.

In this world and certainly in eternal life, the restoration of heaven is our hope. There, we will be made whole in the presence of God.

The Justice of Heaven

> Not everyone who says to me, "Lord, Lord," will enter the kingdom of heaven, but the one who does the will of my Father who is in heaven. On that day many will say to me, "Lord, Lord, did we not prophesy in your name, and cast out demons in your name, and do many mighty works in your name?" And then will I declare to them, "I never knew you; depart from me, you workers of lawlessness." (Matthew 7:21–23)

And what of the consequences? What is the alternative to heaven? Jesus says this will be a place with weeping and gnashing of teeth. Weeping indicates sadness, and gnashing of teeth indicates anger. This is the alternative: sadness and anger.

Heaven is a place of justice. It is not the sort of justice we find here on earth, constantly disappointed by poor decision-making and disagreeing on what should or should not be done to those who commit crimes. Instead, it is a place of pure and perfect justice, a place where only those who have been given Christ's robes of righteousness will dwell. With that in mind, we can be confident there is no room for evil or wickedness. There is no room for disobedient hearts.

Do we want to reach heaven only to be turned away? Do we

want to live a false faith here in the world and convince ourselves that the nagging convictions we are facing don't matter?

If we are not living according to the truth of Scripture, we will be told to depart. He will say he never knew us. This isn't meant to bring up fear or insecurity about our salvation. Honestly, most people who care about whether or not they are actually saved are probably willing to dig deep enough to find the assurance of it. These verses strike fear into many hearts, but they don't have to.

Do you believe Jesus is the only way to God? Do you believe you are a sinner in need of a Savior? Have you been justified by turning to Christ? Are you being sanctified by daily allowing the Holy Spirit to work in your heart? Do you believe in the foundations of Scripture, the Trinity, and that you are saved by faith through grace alone?

Many creeds and covenants out there can help us in the foundations of our faith, but ultimately, if we are walking daily with God and living a life that is devoted to his will, we shouldn't be living in fear. We know God is good in all his glory. And we know he is merciful and gracious.

We do not sin that grace may abound, but we do repent for our failures and seek to be sanctified and restored so that we no longer fall into those habits (Romans 6:1–4). If we do not, the consequences are too great. We go back to the question of what consequences we prefer: suffering for our faith in this world or spending eternity apart from God.

Heaven is a place of justice and as a result, we have to know where our hearts truly lie. If we are going to seek God, we must do so with all that is in us.

Worth It

It's worth the sacrifice. Look back through the pitfalls and the questions at the end of each chapter. Is heaven worth it to lay down those fears? Is Jesus worth standing up for? Is eternity more valuable than the comfort of tomorrow?

If so, you know what you need to do. You know where your heart lies and where to go from here. We have looked at some extremely practical steps to take that will propel you forward in the journey of boldness. We've acknowledged that failures happen, and you should feel condemned if you fail sometimes. But if you're going to live this life, take the steps. Do what needs to be done.

And live a bold life that leads to a merciful, restorative, and just eternity.

Be bold, not belligerent.

For Reflection

1. The chapter talks about a life of boldness leading to eternity with God. How does the thought of an eternal reward in heaven motivate you to live boldly for Christ today? How can this eternal perspective reshape your actions and decisions in the present?

2. What is the significance of Nebuchadnezzar's story of restoration in heaven? How does this story give you hope that God can restore and use anyone, regardless of their past?

3. Matthew 7:21–23 warns about the danger of false faith. How does this challenge you to evaluate the authenticity of your own relationship with God?

4. What do you think the consequences are of living a false faith, both in this life and in the next? How can you ensure that your faith remains rooted in truth and aligned with God's purposes for your life?

5. The chapter talks about the worth of heaven and asks whether it's worth laying down fears and comforts for eternity. What fears or comforts are you holding onto that might be hindering you from living boldly for Christ? Is the hope of heaven worth the sacrifice?

Teaching Kids

Throughout this book, we've looked at our personal responsibility to live a bold life that stands up for truth in accordance with Scripture. But for those with children or who hope to one day have them, this is only one part of our responsibility.

Our lives should be an example to others, no matter who they are, to show what it looks like to have a firm grasp of truth. We want others around us to see our witness and our willingness to sacrifice for it.

But with our children, we must actively be teaching them the truth. We have to understand how to disciple them. Croft M. Pentz said, "Our children are the only possessions we can take to Heaven."[82] While the word *possessions* may rub people the wrong way, he's absolutely right. We cannot bring anything else in this world that is precious to us to heaven. But our children are precious to us, and it is our duty to prepare the soil of their souls and sow the seeds of truth.

Only the Holy Spirit can do the work of bringing them to Jesus, but we have a deep responsibility to raise them with the knowledge of truth and in the spirit of boldness. We have to teach them how to direct their willfulness and determination toward a passion for

---

[82] Croft M. Pentz, *The Complete Book of Zingers* (Tyndale House Publishers, 2002), 232.

righteousness.

In *The Last Battle*, C. S. Lewis writes of Aslan and Lucy:

Lucy said, "We're so afraid of being sent away, Aslan. And you have sent us back into our own world so often." "No fear of that," said Aslan. "Have you not guessed?" Their hearts leapt, and a wild hope rose within them. "There was a real railway accident," said Aslan softly. "Your father and mother and all of you are—as you used to call it in the Shadowlands—dead. The term is over: the holidays have begun. The dream is ended: this is the morning."83

We want our children to be with us in the Shadowlands. Just as there are practical steps to our own boldness, there are practical steps when discipling our children. And no, this does not include driving them to youth group and picking them up later.

Teach Them Who They Are

"Therefore, if anyone is in Christ, he is a new creation. The old has passed away; behold, the new has come" (2 Corinthians 5:17). While we want our children in church and in Christian circles, and maybe even in a Christian school, it can't stop there. We have a responsibility to teach them who they are.

Our children need to know who they are in Christ, to know that they can shed off the old for the sake of the new. We must teach them the reality of Jesus and that we must depend on his righteousness in place of our own.

Different children will have different personalities, and what works for some may not work for others. Some children will hear and naturally have faith; others will hear and naturally question. Through regular family Bible study, discussing foundational principles of faith, and memorizing verses and/or concepts, we can set a beginning standard. It's never too early to begin training our children in biblical ideas. Even if they are too young to understand what they hear or memorize, it will open the doors for deeper discussions when they are ready and when they do have questions.

A four-year-old child can learn about the Trinity and have very

---

83 C. S. Lewis, *The Last Battle*, (HarperCollins Children's Books, 2023).

little understanding of what it means and how we can possibly have one God with three distinct persons. In truth, adult Christians can't even properly wrap our minds around this concept. But we can explain to them that for now, it's okay to have questions and just have faith that it's true. As they get older, we can discuss it further and what the church has had to say about the Trinity over the past few thousand years. We can ultimately come to agree that we don't want a God who fits in our brains anyway, so we don't need to fear a little confusion.

If our children are in Christ, they can lean on him for redemption, even if they don't entirely understand the nitty-gritty of deeper theological concepts. Identity is a deeply rooted question that has become more prominent as culture has grown ever more individualistic. Today, we argue over identity politics. Everyone wants to be special, and they think they are only special if they are distinct from others.

We can show our children the truth when we remind them there is nothing greater than being in Christ and that is where their identity is found. We must also show them our example. We can show that our identity is not in our job, in our ability to put a good meal on the table, or in our looks. It is in Christ alone.

Teach Them How to Defend Their Faith

"Train up a child in the way he should go; even when he is old he will not depart from it" (Proverbs 22:6). The foundations mentioned in the previous section also transfer over to defending our faith and for our children to defend theirs. We have to teach our children what it looks like to stand firm in their faith and how to build a solid foundation. Teach them to ask questions and be a good example of how to answer them. If we don't have an answer, we try to find one. Let them see how to do that themselves as well.

Teach your children apologetics. Let them hear theological truths, debates, and arguments against their faith. Of course, focus on what is age-appropriate so that you don't confuse your children. It wouldn't be wise to let them listen to a debate on gender ideology at four or five years old when they don't really understand what gender even means. After all, there's a reason gender culture likes to target kindergarteners.

But if you know your child well and spend a lot of time

investing in them, you will know what they are ready for and when. As they grow, let them dig deeper. Surround them with truth so that they know the truth so well that they can't help but spot the lies.

Be Warned

There is absolutely a cultural war against families, and the surgeon general has even issued a warning about the mental health and stress levels of parents.[84] You know there's a problem when a command to populate the earth in Genesis 1:28 is replaced with the idea that parenthood is a public health emergency. Along with all the other depopulation pushes, the powers that be don't want families anymore.

More and more people are putting off having children for financial reasons. More and more are choosing to be child-free altogether. And with gender ideology, more and more children are doing irreversible damage to their bodies that will prevent them from ever having children, even if they want them or change their minds later. Because of this, we need to be on alert more than ever and to be aware of what lies our children are being told.

Look for postmodern Marxist and evolutionary thoughts. Are they leaning into identity politics? Are they more focused on justice than truth? Is their idea of justice based on important, worthwhile issues, or is it based on the latest cultural trend?

Don't be afraid to start the conversation and ask them hard questions. We don't need to let our children lead the way on this. We can challenge them with apologetics and truly encourage them to think beyond the foundations we have tried to lay.

If your child can't come up with an answer as to why the world's message is wrong, look at it together in Scripture. And if they have already been influenced by the world and they try to argue with you about it, humbly show them where they're missing the point, and then direct them toward the truth.

Talk about these issues and explain why it is wrong to hold themselves to the standard of the world instead of diving into

---

[84] "U.S. Surgeon General Issues Advisory on the mental health and well-being of parents," August 28, 2024, HHS.gov, https://www.hhs.gov/about/news/2024/08/28/us-surgeon-general-issues-advisory-mental-health-well-being-parents.html.

Scripture for answers. Don't be afraid of the messy, difficult conversations. Even if your child is struggling to grasp what the world is telling them versus what the Bible says, hold firm to truth and challenge them while still showing grace and not rolling your eyes as the wise parent of the foolish child.

If you just aren't sure about a certain issue, you can, "I don't know." Look up the answer together. Go to a trusted pastor with your child and ask to discuss the matter.

Our children are worth it. Their eternity is worth it. Love them enough to inconvenience yourself and take the time to train them up and disciple them as the Bible commands.

Boldly be a better parent and boldly love your children into eternity.

www.ingramcontent.com/pod-product-compliance
Lightning Source LLC
Chambersburg PA
CBHW051415090426
42737CB00014B/2686